BEST PRACTICES
FOR YOGA IN THE
CRIMINAL JUSTICE SYSTEM

BEST PRACTICES FOR YOGA IN THE CRIMINAL JUSTICE SYSTEM

Presented by the Yoga Service Council
and the Omega Institute

EDITOR

Carol Horton, Ph.D

CONTRIBUTING EDITORS

Bill Brown, PRYT, C-IAYT, RYT-200; Mary Lynn Fitton, RN, MS, FNP;
Sarahjoy Marsh, MA, E-RYT-500; Kath Meadows, MA, E-RYT-500;
Danielle Rousseau, PHD, LMHC; Rosa Vissers, MFA, E-YT-500

CONTRIBUTORS

Bob Altman, RYT-200; Susanna Barkataki, MED, E-RYT; Leslie Booker;
Denise Davidson; Toni DeMarco, MS, MFT; Marshawn Feltus;
Jennifer Cohen Harper, MA, E-RYT, RCYT; Gabrielle Prisco, MA, ESQ.;
Michael Huggins, MBA, E-RYT; Jill Weiss Ippolito, RYT;
De Jur Jones, C-IAYT, RYT-200; Sue Jones; Brianne Murphy Cerdán, BA, E-RYT;
Charlene A. Sams, E-RYT, CRYT; Jessica Stolley, MS, LMHP, LDAC;
Kathryn Monti Thomas, E-RYT, RCYT; Kimberleigh Weiss-Lewit, MA, RYT 500, CD/CDT

REVIEWERS

James Fox, MA; Hala Khouri, MA, SEP, E-RYT; Anneke Lucas, EW-RYT-500;
Mary Ellen Mastrorilli, PHD; Laura Sygrove, MSW, RYT-500

Note to Readers

All the findings and conclusions reported in this book are those of the editor, contributing editors, contributors, and reviewers, who are solely responsible for its contents. No statement in this document should be construed as an official position of any U.S. public agency, department, or institution. *Best Practices for Yoga in the Criminal Justice System* is intended to serve as a supplement to yoga teacher trainings and professional education programs, licensures, and/or accreditations, not as a substitute for them.

Cover image: Men's yoga and meditation class led by Charlene A. Sams, *Best Practices for Yoga in the Criminal Justice System* contributor and Yoga Service Council board member, at the George Hill Correctional Facility in Thornton, Pennsylvania.

Photo credit: Larry Kuhn, Larry Kuhn Photography, 2017

© 2017 Yoga Service Council
YSC-Omega Publications
PO Box 8238. Atlanta GA 31106-0238
Contact: board@yogaservicecouncil.org

ISBN-10: 1979840393
ISBN-13: 978-1979840392

CONTENTS

Welcome to the Third Yoga Service Best Practices Book

Thank you for your interest in the latest edition of the Yoga Service Best Practices series, a joint project of the Yoga Service Council (YSC) and Omega Institute. As the third book in this collection, *Best Practices for Yoga in the Criminal Justice System* represents the collective wisdom of the tremendously talented and dedicated people who contributed to it, as well as who worked tirelessly on the first two guides in the series: *Best Practices for Yoga in Schools* and *Best Practices for Yoga with Veterans*. From these devoted individuals, much was learned about the process of collaborative writing (and thinking!) that we have undertaken.

The Yoga Service Council is a nonprofit organization dedicated to the vision of a world where everyone has equal access to yoga and mindfulness practices that support healing, resilience, self-development, community building, and positive social change. As a membership organization, we support individuals and organizations working to make yoga accessible to all, through an annual conference, resources such as this book, webinars, mentorships, and other offerings.

When this series originated, the goal was to create resources that could cross the boundaries of various programs, curriculums, and organizations. We worked to gather the wisdom and experience of a broad range of professionals to synthesize ideas in such a way as to make them maximally useful to both the field as a whole and to the individuals who engage with these guides. After three full iterations of this process, I am confident that we have exceeded the expectations of the initial idea, and that the work done on this and previous guides in the series is of exemplary quality. As such, it has the potential to significantly support those in the field of yoga service as well as the many allied professionals working to bring these empowering tools to all.

The Best Practices series is dedicated to uplifting the field of yoga service by sharing the insights, experiences, and knowledge of leading teachers, researchers, therapists, medical professionals, policymakers, and others. With each project, we gather 25 experts in person for a working week at the Omega Institute. The creation of the book unfolds during an 18-month process of conversation, integration, and review. We have been fortunate to have Carol Horton, YSC board vice president, serving as the editor of both this guide and *Best Practices for Yoga with Veterans*. Carol has skillfully woven the perspectives of many, along with the nuances of this complex material, into an easy-to-engage-with book that beautifully balances depth and accessibility.

We are grateful to our many contributors, contributing editors, and peer reviewers for sharing their knowledge. Gratitude as well goes to Kathryn Thomas, who as project organizer did a wonderful job of bringing the group together, and to the YSC Board of Directors, which worked toward its success in different ways. The support of lululemon and its Here to Be program has been a significant factor in the success of the series. Many individuals at the Omega Institute invested in this work, including Robert "Skip" Backus, Carol Donahoe, Kathleen Laucius, and Mark Lerner. And, of course, each of the individuals who contributed to this effort was supported by and has learned from countless others, including and especially the students, who with courageous hearts have engaged even when the reasons to disengage have been plenty.

The mission of the Yoga Service Council is to maximize the effectiveness, sustainability, and impact of individuals and organizations working to make yoga and mindfulness practices equally accessible to all. In generating this resource, that mission was never far from our minds. Bringing yoga into the criminal justice system is a challenging proposition with many potential pitfalls. The wisdom compiled in this guide represents many years of hard-earned knowledge. Our hope is that sharing it enables others to go forward with a strong sense of both the opportunities and challenges of this work, to offer programming that lives up to its enormous potential, and to support the unlimited potential of the people serving and served.

With gratitude,

Jennifer Cohen Harper
YSC Board President

A MESSAGE FROM THE OMEGA INSTITUTE

Since our beginning, Omega's mission has been to awaken the best in the human spirit and to provide hope and healing for individuals and society. Yoga and service have always been core components of our offering, and they continue to serve as transformative tools toward our personal and collective growth and well-being.

Over the years, an ever-widening network of people and organizations that share our deep commitment to service has enriched our community. Through this experience, we have learned that the power of working together is much stronger than walking the path alone. When we combine our energy and intentions, we extend our reach and have a greater positive impact in the world. That's why it's only natural that the Yoga Service Council and Omega have partnered together on a path to offer and support yoga service.

This partnership began in 2009, when Omega offered space for a group of yoga teachers to come together and talk about ways to support those who work with vulnerable and underserved populations. The YSC emerged from this initial gathering and offered the first annual Yoga Service Conference at Omega in 2011.

During each Yoga Service Conference at Omega, we have discovered and redis- covered that the YSC Board of Directors and others who choose to be involved in this work are some of the most compassionate people we have met. Yoga service truly is a practice of the heart—and a specific path of yoga that fully aligns with Omega's mission and ideals.

As a result of our shared commitment to yoga and service, the YSC and Omega decided to formally partner in 2014 to bring yoga into the lives of more individuals and communities that have limited access to these vital teachings. We are excited to continue this partnership with the YSC and all its member organizations.

One example of our partnership is this book, the third title in our Yoga Service Best Practices series. *Best Practices for Yoga in the Criminal Justice System* began in 2016 when more than 20 leaders committed to integrating yoga into the criminal justice system came together at Omega for a week of shared reflection, discussion, and community building. Helping people who are either involved or working in the criminal justice system learn to use yoga and mindfulness to support holistic health and well-being resonates deeply with Omega's mission of awakening the best in the human spirit and of providing hope and healing for individuals and society.

We offer a special thanks to Yoga in the Criminal Justice System project leaders Kathryn Monti Thomas (project manager) and Carol Horton (writer and editor), as well as the entire YSC Board for their important work in the world. We're honored to be your partners on this journey.

With deep appreciation,

Robert "Skip" Backus
Chief Executive Officer
Omega Institute

EDITOR'S INTRODUCTION

In popular culture, yoga has become widely associated with images of pretty young white women serenely performing impressive gymnastic poses. Such pop imagery is starkly at odds with the harsh realities of the U.S. criminal justice system, which people across the political spectrum agree is highly dysfunctional in ways that disproportionately impact low-income men of color. Given this disjuncture, it would be understandable if readers as yet unaware of the invaluable work being done with yoga in the criminal justice system might see the basic premise of *Best Practices for Yoga in the Criminal Justice System* as oddly implausible at best.

If that's the case, it's my fervent hope that such readers engage with this book sufficiently to learn that yoga has nothing to do with what one looks like, how physically fit and flexible one is, or what one's life circumstances may be. Despite today's misleading pop messaging, yoga remains a practice that teaches us how to work with the mind, breath, body, and life force in ways that foster healing, resilience, self-awareness, self-regulation, compassion, nonviolence, and positive change. As such, it's a practice that has much to offer people in the criminal justice system, including those who are incarcerated or otherwise system-involved and those who work as correctional officers, administrators, or other criminal justice professionals.

While it may run counter to common assumptions, promoting yoga in the criminal justice system is a project that makes perfect sense. The criminal justice context is exceedingly stressful. Research shows yoga to be exceptionally effective at reducing the negative impacts of stress, which is vitally important to both physical and psychological health. Particularly when chronic, stress can negatively impact all of our physiological systems (cardiovascular, respiratory, gastrointestinal, endocrine, immune, musculoskeletal, etc.), as well as our mental health and emotional resilience. Research indicates that regular yoga practice reduces symptoms of anxiety, depression, and post-traumatic stress, as well as heart rate and systolic blood pressure. In the process, it increases overall physical fitness, flexibility, balance, and endurance (Bullock, n.d.).

Although relatively little research has focused on yoga in the criminal justice system, what has been done affirms that it can help incarcerated people with mood and anxiety disorders, substance abuse, stress, impulsivity, and a wide range of physiological concerns (Muirhead and Fortune, 2016). One set of in-depth interviews with eight formerly incarcerated men who participated in a prison yoga program for 2 to 10 years found that yoga enabled them to reduce and manage issues of depression, anxiety, aggression, and addiction, while helping with a wide range of physical ailments (particularly, but not exclusively, back pain). At the same time, yoga increased their self-awareness, self-regulation, emotional intelligence, relationship management, social awareness, and dedication to community. Despite repeated prompting, study participants reported no negative impacts of their yoga participation at all (Viorst, 2017).

Providing a meaningful opportunity to realize such positive benefits, however, requires that whatever yoga instruction may be offered has been adapted as necessary to be appropriate for a criminal justice context. Yoga is an unregulated and nonstandardized field, with an enormously wide range of practices included under the umbrella term "yoga." In this book and in the Best Practices series of which it's a part, we use the word "yoga" to refer to those that include postures and movement, breath work, focused attention, and deep relaxation. Although we recognize that the yoga tradition has other vital dimensions, such as philosophical and ethical study, they are outside the purview of this work.

Even this more circumscribed definition of yoga encompasses a very wide and diverse range of particular styles and methods. Given this variety, it shouldn't be assumed that it's okay to offer just any type of class in a criminal justice setting. Some common ways of teaching would not be appropriate or even safe in this context. Potential problems include physical injuries caused by an overly strenuous practice and psychological upset caused by teaching that is not trauma-informed.

It's vital that yoga service providers who wish to work in the criminal justice system receive appropriate training and support. Otherwise, they risk causing harm to students they wish to serve while unintentionally undermining the goal of promoting yoga in the criminal justice system as a whole. *Best Practices for Yoga in the Criminal Justice System* provides an accessible yet detailed overview of how best to teach yoga in this context, as well as how to build and sustain yoga service organizations dedicated to working there. While the particularities can and should vary, overall this means that the yoga offered must be safe, effective, trauma-informed, gender responsive, age appropriate, culturally sensitive, and aligned with institutional rules and regulations.

Yoga service providers range from solo teachers to well-developed organizations capable of running multiple programs at different sites, serving on multidisciplinary teams, coordinating post-release services, and more. Regardless of size and capacity, providers should be proficient in trauma-informed yoga (TIY) and able to work in a criminal justice setting effectively.

While written for a general audience, *Best Practices for Yoga in the Criminal Justice System* is intended to be of particular interest to:

1. Yoga teachers, programs, and organizations interested in serving this population;

2. Department of Corrections (DOC) administrators seeking to learn about, establish, and/or improve existing yoga programs;

3. Correctional officers and other criminal justice professionals curious about how yoga might be helpful to them, either personally or in their work environment;

4. Judges, probation officials, policymakers, and others interested in how yoga programs might contribute to better system functioning and outcomes;

5. System-based medical care and mental health providers interested in yoga's potential as a complementary health modality;

6. Scholars and policy researchers seeking to deepen their knowledge of what sort of yoga works best in a criminal justice setting; and

7. Incarcerated and otherwise system-involved people who'd like to learn more about how and why yoga can be a meaningful personal and community resource.

Although this book primarily focuses on work with system-involved adults, many if not most of the best practices presented are relevant to working with youth. Special considerations for young people are flagged throughout. Several sections discuss youth issues in-depth. That said, readers who work with youth, as well as with any distinct adult population, are encouraged to tailor these recommendations as necessary to support the population they serve.

Best Practices for Yoga in the Criminal Justice System integrates the experience, insights, and knowledge of more than 25 leaders in this emerging field. Together, the contributors, editors, and reviewers who co-created this book have expertise not only in yoga, mindfulness, and meditation but also in nursing, behavioral health, adolescent and women's health, recovery services, suicide prevention, clinical psychotherapy, family systems, child welfare, youth development, youth justice, corrections, intergenerational trauma, neuroscience, crisis response, victim advocacy, and more. Each of the book's 22 contributors generously volunteered their time to be part of a collaborative process that demanded a week of in-person engagement at the Omega Institute plus a year-and-a-half's worth of work.

Many thanks are due to those who made *Best Practices for Yoga in the Criminal Justice System* possible by generously sharing their time, expertise, and support.

First to thank are our contributors, who collectively generated the core content for this work. Special thanks are due to the six people in this group who also served as contributing editors, drafting core segments of the text. Equal thanks must be extended to our five external reviewers, who donated their time to provide feedback on the draft manuscript and make the final product even better. A very special thanks is due to Project Manager Kathryn Monti Thomas, who organized the Best Practices Symposium at Omega that laid the groundwork for this book. Everyone involved benefited from her hard work and dedication, which made that foundational experience the best it could possibly be.

Best Practices for Yoga in the Criminal Justice System could not have been written without the generous support of the Omega Institute and lululemon's Here to Be program. We at the Yoga Service Council are deeply grateful for our ongoing partnership with Omega, which enables us to pursue our passion for yoga service in ways we could never replicate otherwise. We are also thankful and proud to be part of lululemon's efforts to support, unite, and amplify the work of the yoga service community. With the continued support of these two primary partners, the YSC Board of Directors, and our many sustaining, organizational, and individual members, we look forward to bringing you the next book in this series, *Best Practices for Yoga for Sexual Trauma Survivors*, in 2018.

It's been an honor for me personally to work on this book in conjunction with so many inspiring individuals and organizations. Based on my own experience teaching yoga to women in Cook County Jail, as well as what I've learned through years of personal study and practice, I see the work of integrating yoga into the criminal justice system as a shared project with unlimited positive potential. It's my heartfelt hope that this book builds on the good work already being done to make this healing and potentially transformative practice universally available both within the system and beyond.

Now more than ever, I'm inspired by the Yoga Service Council's vision of "a world where everyone has equal access to yoga and mindfulness practices that support healing, resilience, self-development, community building, and positive social change." I believe this book can play an important role in moving that aspirational hope closer toward everyday lived reality. That said, I'm well aware that this project requires sustained collective effort to move forward—and that it's not easy.

I hope readers find this work not only informative and useful but also a source of inspiration for new or continued engagement with our shared project of integrating yoga into the criminal justice system further. This work has already brought more healing, hope, and justice into the system—and, by extension, into the lives of countless individuals and their families and communities. Now it's time to build on the strong foundation that's been laid. We warmly invite you to join us in this endeavor and explore its multifaceted benefits and possibilities for yourself.

Warmly,

Carol Horton, PhD
Vice President, Yoga Service Council

1

CULTURE AND COMMUNICATION

Yoga teachers and yoga service organizations should be aware of and sensitive to the cultural sensibilities and communication styles of the people and organizations they work with. True in any context, this is particularly critical when offering yoga in the high-stakes, high-stress environment of the criminal justice system. Of course, cultural norms vary among different national systems, as well as within the various facilities, divisions, and programs of each. This book is based on the experience of teaching yoga in the U.S. criminal justice system, and the following discussion reflects this fact. Readers concerned with other countries can nonetheless benefit from it by adapting the general principles presented to their specific national context.

Wherever a criminal justice system is located, its overall structure—as well as the core social, political, and economic challenges it confronts—exerts a powerful influence on the particular cultures that develop within it. At the same time, there is always significant variation throughout any given system depending on the individuals involved in its different subsections and locations. Leadership is especially important. Wardens, superintendents, and other administrators who oversee facility operations and programs can powerfully impact particular organizational cultures.

Yoga service providers should strive to understand the structure of the system they're working with and the challenges it confronts, while developing relationships with local leadership and staff. To be effective, these and other processes of learning should be ongoing and integrated into concomitant processes of self-reflection and self-inquiry. Teaching yoga in the criminal justice system requires the capacity to critically examine one's own social position, including whatever privileges it confers or biases it instills. Humility and a willingness to learn are indispensible if yoga is to be taught effectively as a healing practice that serves to support the people working or living in what is all too often an alienating, dehumanizing, and dangerous environment.

CULTURE AND COMMUNICATION: UNDERSTAND SYSTEM STRUCTURE

Yoga service providers should understand the basic structure of the criminal justice system.

The U.S. criminal justice system is complex, with distinct federal, state, local, and military divisions. Although yoga service providers cannot be expected to understand the entire system in detail, they're encouraged to have a basic grasp of the following:

- the difference between federal, state, and local jurisdictions;

- the difference between prisons, jails, and problem-solving or specialty courts;

- the difference between low-, medium-, and high-security prisons;

- basics of the U.S. immigration detention system;

- basic differences between the adult and youth systems;

- basic progression of criminal cases from pretrial status to plea bargain or trial, sentencing or acquittal, and, if utilized, probation and parole.[1]

---

1   The U.S. Department of Justice provides information on the progression of criminal cases in the federal system on its website ("Steps in the Federal Criminal Process," https://www.justice. gov/usao/justice-101/steps-federal-criminal-process).

Yoga service providers cannot be expected to become experts in the criminal justice system, which is vast, complex, variegated, and sometimes difficult for even experts to understand thoroughly. Developing a basic understanding of the overall system and how the particular part they're working in fits into it, however, is crucial.

Without such grounding in basic facts of the system, it is impossible for providers to have any realistic understanding of the particularity of their own social positions vis-à-vis the students they intend to serve. This knowledge is necessary for effective teaching, as it provides a necessary foundation for realizing the core yoga service commitment to "conscious relationship" (see chapter 4, "Relationship Building").

It is beyond the scope of this book to provide a thorough briefing on U.S. criminal justice system structure. As discussed in chapter 2, "Training and Staffing," yoga service organizations and individual teachers need to make sure that they receive appropriate training on this and other issues before beginning to teach. The following discussion of system parameters is provided simply to give readers who are unfamiliar with them some background so that reading the rest of the book may be more fruitful.

Federal Bureau of Prisons (FBOP). The federal prison system incarcerates people convicted of violating federal laws. Key types of federal facilities include: *(1) federal prison camps* (minimum-security prisons), *(2) federal correctional institutions* (low-security prisons), *(3) federal medium-security prisons, (4) U.S. penitentiaries* (high-security prisons with very secure boundaries),[2] *(5) correctional complex institutions* (purpose and security level varies), and *(6) Residential Drug Abuse Program (RDAP)* (intensive treatment program for offenders with substance use disorders; sentences usually lasts nine months) (Jull n.d.).

---

2   The FBOP explains the different security levels of the facilities it operates and provides lists of each on its website ("About Our Facilities," https://www.bop.gov/about/facilities/federal_prisons.jsp).

In 2014, half of those incarcerated in federal prisons were drug offenders. Thirty-six percent were there for violations of public order (immigration, weapons, and other). Only seven percent were there for violent crimes (Sentencing Project 2017).

Both federal and state prisons segregate incarcerated people by biologically defined sex, usually in separate prisons.

State Prisons. State prisons are intended to incarcerate people convicted of a felony under state law. As in the federal system, there are different types of facilities with different security levels. State-controlled prison systems have traditionally been seen as more dangerous than their federal counterparts, as they're more likely to house people convicted of violent crimes. (In 2014, 53 percent of people in state prison were convicted of violent crimes.) Some states, such as New York, require those in prison to spend the majority of their sentence in maximum-security prisons. Some state prisons are built and administered by private companies (Cartmell, n.d.).

Jails. Jails are operated by local law enforcement authorities and intended to confine people before or after adjudication. In practice, this means that many people detained in jail have been charged with an offense, but their cases have not yet gone through the process of being settled, dismissed, or tried. For example, more than 90 percent of individuals admitted to Chicago's Cook County Jail are pretrial detainees. Frequently, this means that they are incarcerated following a bond hearing because they are low-income and unable to pay their required bond.

A minority have been sentenced and are serving some term of incarceration. Although state laws vary, jail sentences are supposed to be relatively short (e.g., from less than a year to 2.5 years maximum, depending on the state). In some jurisdictions, however, people are serving significantly longer sentences. In 2011, for example, California began incarcerating people convicted of nonviolent crimes in local jails, rather than in state prisons, in response to chronic prison overcrowding.[3] As a result, the average jail stay increased from a few months to more than a year.

The size of jails varies tremendously. The smallest size category tracked by the U.S. Bureau of Justice Statistics has a capacity of 49 or fewer people. The nation's largest, Cook County Jail, admits approximately 100,000 detainees annually and averages a daily population of 9,000 (CCDC, n.d.). In 2015, large jail jurisdictions with 2,500 or more incarcerated held 21 percent of the total jail population. On an average day in 2015, an estimated 721,300 inmates were confined in county and city jails in the United States (Minton & Zeng, 2016).

Wagner (2015) reports that 11 million people cycle though the nation's 3,283 jails annually.

Problem-Solving Courts. Problem-solving courts are intended to address underlying problems that contribute to behaviors associated with incarceration. They are typically diversionary, meaning that participants agree to follow court-imposed guidelines in order to avoid prosecution, incarceration, or other typical criminal justice outcomes. In 2012, there were 3,052 problem-solving courts in the United States, primarily drug courts (44 percent) and mental health courts (11 percent).

Drug courts are supposed to provide a comprehensive therapeutic experience from the time after a person's arrest to when he or she completes parole or probation. A treatment team composed of a judge, lawyers, case managers, health providers, and therapists works with the defendant to provide effective treatment and ensure legal compliance. Drug courts can require stays at detox centers,

---

3   The policy change of reducing overcrowding was mandated by the U.S. Supreme Court, which ruled in 2011 that California's prison system amounted to "cruel and unusual punishment" and required the state to reduce its overall population from 181 percent of capacity to 137.5 percent in two years, or about 33,000 people incarcerated. The California legislature then passed a "re-alignment plan" in which prisoners convicted of nonviolent, non-sex-related, and nonserious crimes could be returned to their original counties for either time in the county jail or parole. State statistic show that savings from the reduced prison population totaled $453 million in 2012 alone, with no adverse effect on the overall safety of Californians (Jackman, 2016).

inpatient rehab programs, outpatient therapy, self-help groups, and a variety of other treatment services. They may also require community service hours, completion of vocational training, and proof of abstinence through regular drug tests (DrugRehab.com, n.d.; CSDP, n.d.).

Youth Justice System. Each state and the District of Columbia has its own laws that govern its youth justice system. How youth courts operate may also vary from county to county and municipality to municipality within a state. The federal government has jurisdiction over only a small number of youths, such as those who commit crimes on Indian reservations or in national parks.

To be eligible for youth court, a young person must be a considered a "juvenile" under state law. While this varies by state, it is most commonly encompasses those ages 14 to 18. Youth courts have a broad range of sentencing options, including incarceration in a youth detention facility, house arrest, and alternatives that do not involve confinement such as counseling, curfews, and probation (Michon, n.d.; IM/NRC, 2001).

Immigration Detention Centers. The United States operates the world's largest immigration detention system, with approximately 30,000 people detained in some 200 facilities on any given day. Detention facilities include jails, private facilities, field offices, youth detention centers, and "family residential centers." The size and cost of U.S. immigration detention and removal operations have spiraled since 1990 and now total approximately $19 billion annually (Global Detention Project, 2016).

Probation. In criminal law, probation is a period of supervision over someone who has been convicted of an offense ordered by a court in lieu of serving time in prison. In some jurisdictions, the term "probation" applies only to community sentences (alternatives to incarceration) such as suspended sentences. In others, it also includes supervision of those conditionally released from prison on parole. People on probation are ordered to follow certain conditions set forth by the court, often under the supervision of a probation officer. They can be incarcerated if judged to break the rules set by the court or probation officer (BJS, n.d.).

Parole. In criminal law, those on parole refer to people who have been convicted of an offense, incarcerated, and conditionally released to serve the remaining portion of their sentence. Incarcerated people may be released to parole either by a parole board decision or according to provisions of a statute. Parolees can have a number of different supervision statuses, including active supervision—which means they are required to regularly report to a parole authority in person, by mail, or by telephone—and inactive status, which means they are excluded from regularly reporting. Parolees are typically required to fulfill certain conditions and adhere to specific rules of conduct; failure to comply can result in a return to incarceration (BJS, n.d.).

CULTURE AND COMMUNICATION: UNDERSTAND INSTITUTIONAL CONTEXT

Yoga service providers should understand the structure and culture of the particular facility or program they're working in.

The organizational culture of a facility or program is impacted by both the national- and state-level systems of which it's a part and the particular people, procedures, habits, and norms that influence its day-to-day operations. As noted earlier, wardens, superintendents, and other administrators who oversee facilities and/or programs can play a particularly important role in developing different organizational cultures. Yoga service providers should strive to understand the context they are working in on both these macro and micro levels. Although they cannot be expected to become criminal justice experts, having a basic grounding in the local, state, and federal systems provides an important foundation for culturally sensitive and responsive work.

It is important for yoga teachers to understand that criminal justice professionals see their primary responsibility as the maintenance of public safely. From their perspective, this means that security procedures take precedence over everything else. Often, standard security protocols are inconvenient for yoga teachers and others who enter and exit facilities in order to provide classes and other programming. For example, there may be strict entrance procedures and/or delays bringing students to class on time. Yoga service providers need to be prepared to accept such occurrences as a normal part of working in this environment, and they should defer to system professionals and staff on safety and security measures.

Trainings. Specialized trainings are a primary means of laying this vital groundwork. Ideally, these will be provided by both the facility or program and the yoga service organization itself. (For a more detailed discussion of training issues, see chapter 2, "Training and Staffing.")

Many jurisdictions within the U.S. criminal justice system require all external contractors or volunteers to take an orientation training before beginning their work. The substance and duration of these trainings vary tremendously, ranging from multiple days of in-depth instruction to nothing at all. Yoga service providers should be aware of what, if anything, is offered through the facility or program they're working in; providers should require all volunteers and staff to take it.

As yoga service organizations mature, they should develop in-house trainings to supplement whatever is required by the facility or program. (For a sense of how this step fits into an overall trajectory of yoga service organizational development, see Appendix B.) These trainings might emphasize culture and communications issues most relevant to local yoga instruction, among other topics. They ought to serve as a means of distilling important information learned from study and direct experience, and of passing it on to new teachers and staff. Curriculum should be updated regularly as new lessons are learned and insights gained.

Newer or smaller yoga service organizations that lack the capacity to develop an in-depth training are encouraged to consider compiling a resource list of books and articles instead. Materials that pertain to local issues should be featured to the greatest extent possible. A moderated, closed social media group dedicated to sharing collective knowledge, experience, and resource suggestions can also be an important resource for providers without the ability to develop a training.

In some areas, more established yoga service providers may have relevant training programs that could be joined or adapted with permission. In all cases, it is a good idea to find out what, if any, training options exist locally.

Policy Updates. Laws and policies governing the criminal justice system can and do change regularly at the national, state, and local levels. If possible, yoga service organizations should seek to stay current with relevant changes and update their training materials and/or resource lists as needed.

CULTURE AND COMMUNICATION: ADDRESS STAFF RESPECTFULLY

Yoga service providers should understand staff classifications and appropriate terms of address.

Yoga teachers should learn the relevant staffing structures and job titles of whatever facility or program they're working in, and understand proper interpersonal etiquette and terms of address. Again, all this will vary among jurisdictions, facilities, and divisions. Consequently, it's best for yoga service organizations to develop their own training that covers these issues if possible. As a general rule, the traditional honorifics "Sir" and "Ma'am" may be used to address staff if more-specific titles are not known.

Key Staff. Yoga teachers working in facilities should understand the basic difference between correctional officers, correctional administrators, and civilian staff—and the proper terms of address for each.

Correctional officers, or "COs," are responsible for maintaining security and enforcing rules and regulations inside correctional facilities. Their duties include supervising activity among the incarcerated, searching their cells for weapons and contraband, restraining those who pose a danger to staff and/or other incarcerated people, and controlling disturbances. COs working in state facilities must have at least a high school diploma or GED; some states have additional requirements. Officers working in federal prisons must have a bachelor's degree.

All COs must additionally complete state or departmental training that covers safety and security procedures, correctional laws and policies, self-defense, and weapons. New officers receive on-the-job training from supervising officers at their assigned facilities.

Although there are regional variations in common Department of Corrections (DOC) terminology and lingo, in all cases the term "officer" or "CO" is respectful. In contrast, *the term "guard" is considered demeaning and should not be used.* Failure to address officers correctly can create resentment and distrust.

Correctional administrators have a college degree (typically in criminology and corrections) and/or prior correctional experience. (COs may rise through the ranks to reach an administrative position.) Correctional administrators also receive job-specific training in policies and procedures at the correctional facility where they work. Although administrators may have contact with prisoners, their duties often involve human resource and managerial functions such as supervising correctional staff and managing the prison budget. It is important that yoga teachers learn specific job titles of correctional administrators and use them. Again, in cases where they are uncertain, "Sir" and "Ma'am" are recommended.

Civilian staff include social workers, case managers, mental and medical health providers, volunteer activity coordinators, and so on. Depending on the context, yoga teachers and service organizations may work closely with civilian staff or not at all. They may also interface with correctional officers and administrators through these staff frequently. Given the diversity of this grouping, proper forms of address vary according to professional norms and the nature of the relationship at issue.

Since most prisons have paramilitary structures, it would be wise for yoga teachers to know the rankings of authority, that is: correction officer, corporal, sergeant, lieutenant, captain, and major. While opaque to civilians, these rankings are extremely important to those who work in military or quasi-military settings. Using an incorrect ranking—for example, referring to a captain as an officer—will most likely be perceived as offensive and erodes needed connection and trust.

Being aware of and sensitive to the chain of command among criminal justice professionals and staff—and knowing how to refer to people properly within it—is important.

CULTURE AND COMMUNICATION: ADDRESS SYSTEM-INVOLVED PEOPLE RESPECTFULLY

Yoga service providers should utilize respectful forms of address for system-involved people.

In this book, the term "system-involved" is recommended as a general means of referring to children, youth, and adults who are involved in the criminal justice and related social service systems. This not limited to jails and prisons, and should include youth detention centers and holding facilities, foster care, shelters, alternative/close-to-home facilities, pretrial detention, community corrections and detainment, immigration detention, diagnostic and evaluation centers, forensic hospitals and units, court systems including specialty courts, and reentry facilities.

Yoga service providers should assess what terms constitute respectful forms of address for the incarcerated or otherwise system-involved people they teach and encounter in their work. Similarly, they ought to be respectful when referring to system-involved people when discussing their yoga service work with family, friends, colleagues, and others. Pejorative terms including but not limited to "criminals" should never be used. Yoga teachers are also advised to refrain from adopting any slang terms or informal lingo that they may encounter in this regard.

As teachers get to know their students, the best practice is to learn and refer to them by their preferred personal names. To communicate respect and professionalism, consider using more formal terms of personal address (e.g., Mr. Jones, Ms. Smith). Given the importance of professional hierarchy in criminal justice settings noted above, it is recommended to reserve the non-personalized honorifics of "Sir" and "Ma'am" for staff.

Incarcerated People. How best to refer to incarcerated people depends in part on local culture. Contributors to this book who teach in facilities have had different experiences in this regard. For example, one yoga teacher who had discussed this issue with her students reported that they preferred the term "inmate." Another said that her students liked the directness of the term "prisoner." Still another reported that in her state the proper language was mandated and had recently shifted from "inmate" to "adult [or youth] in custody."

Given that no single term of address is universally preferred, this book follows the findings of an informal survey conducted by The Marshall Project in 2015. It found that 38 percent of 200 respondents prefer "incarcerated person," 23 percent like "prisoner," and roughly 10 percent recommend "inmate" (Hickman, 2015). This preference for "incarcerated person" was in line with that of the contributors to this book and is correspondingly utilized throughout.

Recognition and Respect. Yoga teachers must understand system-involved people as multidimensional human beings who not only have their own personal stories but are highly likely to have been deeply impacted by societal patterns of marginalization and/or discrimination that are much bigger than their own individual lives. Understanding how racial and socioeconomic disparities contribute to problems of mass incarceration is particularly important for yoga teachers who may come to this work with one-dimensional or inaccurate views of incarcerated and other system-involved people.

Being able to appreciate both the uniqueness of each individual, as well as the power of societal patterns to shape people's lives, supports high-quality yoga instruction in that it enables teachers to see the full humanity of their students and to share yoga as a resource that supports their overall health and development as unique human beings.

CULTURE AND COMMUNICATION: UNDERSTAND ISSUES OF MASS INCARCERATION

Yoga service providers should understand why mass incarceration is a critical issue in the United States.

A thorough discussion of the deeply problematic state of the U.S. criminal justice system is far beyond the scope of this book. It is vital, however, that yoga teachers who wish to work in it receive a thorough briefing before beginning to teach and remain dedicated to learning more in the course of their work. Again, yoga service organizations are advised to develop their own training materials that provide a more detailed overview of the system, focusing on their state and local contexts in particular, if and when they have the capacity to do so.

The following discussion of key issues facing the system is intended simply to provide context for this book's ensuing discussion of yoga teaching best practices. Readers should keep in mind that this extremely brief overview cannot take the place of a more thorough training. By the same token, they may remember that the scope of even an excellent training is necessarily limited and that ongoing learning is essential.

Mass Incarceration. The U.S. incarceration rate increased 500 percent during the past four decades and is currently the highest in the world. The U.S. criminal justice system currently holds more than 2.3 million people in 1,719 state prisons, 102 federal prisons, 901 juvenile correctional facilities, 3,163 local jails, and 76 Indian Country[4] jails as well as in military prisons, immigration detention facilities, civil commitment centers, and prisons in the U.S. territories. As noted earlier, 11 million people also churn through American jails every year. In addition, there

---

4   "Indian Country" is a statutory term that includes reservations, pueblos, rancherias, and all lands within Native American reservations, dependent communities, and trust allotments.

are another 840,000 people on parole and 3.7 million on probation (Walmsley, 2015; Wagner, 2015; Wagner & Rabuy, 2017).[5]

Experts believe this enormous increase in U.S. incarceration was primarily driven by legal and policy changes rather than in response to increased crime. Laws passed during the "War on Drugs" in the 1980s caused the numbers of people incarcerated for drug offenses to grow from 41,000 in 1980 to nearly half a million in 2015, an increase of 1,100 percent. More than 31 million people have been arrested for drug offenses since the drug war began. During the same period, mandatory minimum sentencing laws and cutbacks in parole release caused people to be incarcerated for longer periods of time (Sentencing Project, 2017; Alexander, 2012, p. 60).

Racial Disparities. People of color make up 37 percent of the U.S. population but 67 percent of those incarcerated. Black men are six times as likely to be incarcerated as white men. Latino men are more than twice as likely to be incarcerated as white men.

These racial differences cannot be simply attributed to different crime rates. For example, although different racial and ethnic groups in the United States have consistently used and sold drugs at similar rates, three-quarters of all Americans imprisoned for drug offenses have been Black or Latino. Statistically, African Americans are more likely than white Americans to be arrested. Once arrested, they are more likely to be convicted. Once convicted, they are more likely to face stiff sentences. Sentencing policies, implicit racial bias, and socioeconomic inequity contribute to racial disparities at every level of the criminal justice system (Alexander, 2012; Sentencing Project, 2017).

Sex and Gender Disparities. Men and boys are system-involved at radically higher rates than women and girls. Most recent data indicate that approximately 92 percent of people incarcerated in state and federal prisons are male.

---

5   Different states within the state (as opposed to federal) prison system have substantially different incarceration rates. These range from a low of 153 incarcerated per 100,000 in Maine to a high of 818 in Louisiana (Sentencing Project, n.d.).

Women, however, are the fastest-growing segment of the incarcerated population, increasing at nearly double the rate of men since 1985. Today, 1.2 million women are under some form of criminal justice supervision. The number of women incarcerated in state and federal prisons has increased almost eight times during 1980 to 2014, rising from 26,378 to 215,332. More than 60 percent of women in state prisons have a child under the age of 18 (Sentencing Project, 2015).

In the first study of its kind, Meyer et al. (2017) found that "sexual minorities," defined as those who self-identify as lesbian, gay, or bisexual or report a same-sex sexual experience before arrival at the facility, are disproportionately incarcerated. (This research is the most comprehensive currently available regarding how incarceration rates differ by gender and sexual identity. It did not include transgender people.) This includes 9.3 percent of men in prison, 6.2 percent of men in jail, 42.1 percent of women in prison, and 35.7 percent of women in jail. Given that lesbians, gay men, and bisexuals only make up about 3.5 percent of the general U.S. population, these rates are hugely disproportionate, particularly for women.

Economics. Federal and state governments spend $80 billion annually to operate prisons and jails. However, 13.9 percent of corrections costs, such as health care and pension obligations, do not appear in government budgets. When these are included, government spending on corrections totals $91.1 billion. For many state and local governments, these costs have become a serious drain on public resources and effective governance (McLaughlin, Pettus-Davis, Brown, Veeh, & Renn, 2016).

A growing body of research demonstrates that the true cost of incarceration is much more than even this enormous level of direct government spending. Additional social costs borne by incarcerated persons, families, children, and communities include lost wages, higher infant mortality, and increased psychoemotional, educational, and social problems among children and youth of incarcerated parents. When such additional social costs are estimated and aggregated, the cost of incarceration rises to $1.014 trillion, almost 6 percent of GDP (McLaughlin, Pettus-Davis, Brown, Veeh, & Renn, 2016).

As the costs of mass incarceration increase public debt, exacerbate state fiscal crises, and devastate countless individuals, families, and communities, the private prison industry is expanding exponentially. Until the early 1980s, private prisons were virtually nonexistent. During 1990 to 2009, the number of people incarcerated in private prisons increased approximately 1,600 percent. Today, for-profit companies are responsible for approximately 6 percent of state prisoners, 16 percent of federal prisoners, and nearly half of all immigrants detained by the federal government. While these companies claim to assist in reducing public costs and indebtedness, the evidence for this is mixed at best (Shapiro, 2011).

2

TRAINING AND STAFFING

This chapter presents best practices for training yoga teachers and developing yoga teaching staff in a criminal justice context, particularly facilities and court-ordered programs. It is written to be useful to (a) individual yoga teachers, (b) yoga service organizations, and (c) criminal justice professionals.

Individual teachers should find this chapter a useful guide to recommended training options. Yoga service organizations can read it with an eye toward how best to build the organizational capacity and/or partnerships needed to ensure that every teacher is appropriately trained, and that the overall teaching staff is well chosen. Criminal justice professionals may wish to familiarize themselves with its core recommendations in order to build the knowledge base necessary to ask prospective yoga service providers informed questions about teacher training and support.

Key topics covered include: (1) establishing minimum requirements, (2) teaching trauma-informed yoga, (3) addressing secondary trauma, (4) following safety and security procedures, (5) understanding gender and sexuality issues, (6) being aware and fully present, (7) following professional codes of conduct and ethical guidelines, (8) assessing teacher readiness, (9) recruiting a diverse teaching staff, (10) developing diversified teaching teams, and (11) considering cross-gender teaching carefully.

TRAINING AND STAFFING: SET MINIMUM TEACHER TRAINING REQUIREMENTS

DOC administrators, yoga service organizations, and individual teachers should understand and enforce the need to meet specified minimum training requirements.

Yoga service providers should establish minimum training requirements for their teachers and make sure that the requirements are enforced. Start-up organizations and solo teachers should likewise hold themselves accountable for meeting core training standards. Criminal justice professionals interested in facilitating yoga classes should understand why training is important and insist that all teachers meet minimum standards.

Core training recommendations include:

1. **A 200-hour YTT (Yoga Teacher Training) certification or the equivalent** (e.g., a dedicated practice and teaching experience of many years' duration)

2. **Specialized training in trauma-informed yoga or the equivalent** (e.g., professional experience as a social worker or therapist who works with trauma)

3. **Additional yoga training for specialized populations** that form a substantial part of the student body (e.g., youth, pre- and postnatal women, veterans, people with addictions, people with mental health issues, those with physical and/or mental health disabilities, etc.)

Each of these minimum requirements is discussed in more detail below.

200-Hour Credential. Although yoga is a wholly unregulated field in the United States, the 200-hour YTT standard is well established thanks to the influence of Yoga Alliance (YA), a nonprofit organization that sets basic YTT curricular standards. Yoga teachers who complete a YA-approved 200-hour training are eligible to become members of YA and use the widely recognized "RYT-200" designation as a professional credential if they wish. (RYT stands for "Registered Yoga Teacher." A RYT-500 credential also exists for graduates of approved 500-hour programs.)[6]

DOC administrators should be aware that YA provides limited guidance on the development of YTT curricula and does not assess its actual implementation. Similarly, YA does not evaluate individual yoga teachers. This means that the content and quality of 200-hour YTT programs vary significantly. While the RYT-200 credential does carry weight, it is impossible to know precisely what sort of training anyone has received without independent knowledge of the specific program at issue.

Some teachers who have been practicing and teaching yoga for many years may lack a 200-hour certificate yet be exceedingly qualified nonetheless. For this reason, exceptions should be made to the 200-hour YTT requirement, as merited by individual circumstances.

Trauma-Informed Yoga. As detailed below, the incidence of psychological trauma in the criminal justice system is quite high. Consequently, specialized training in the theory and practice of teaching trauma-informed yoga (TIY) should be required for yoga teachers intending to work within it. The only exception to this rule might be yoga teachers with extensive experience working with trauma in other professional contexts such as social work, mental health counseling, or psychotherapy.

TIY is a distinct approach to teaching yoga that tends to be quite different from what's taught in most 200-hour YTTs. Although the specifics of trauma-informed yoga trainings vary, all share the goal of maximizing the therapeutic benefits of the practice for students who have been psychologically and emotionally impacted by trauma, including but not limited to those suffering from PTSD (post-traumatic stress disorder). (TIY focuses on addressing psychoemotional

---

6 The International Association of Yoga Therapy (IAYT) recently developed a yoga therapy certification. While not yet well established, this may soon become a vital credential to consider.

trauma, which may or may not be concurrent with physical trauma.) Often, trauma-informed trainings are developed with a particular population in mind such as homeless youth or domestic violence survivors.

Many TIY trainings suggest practices that are not possible within a prison or jail setting. Prison-focused TIY trainings should address this disparity and incorporate likely environmental conditions and circumstances. If possible, teachers are advised to take a training tailored to serve incarcerated people and the criminal justice system.

When criminal justice–specific trainings are not available, yoga teachers should prioritize what works best for students in that context over general TIY methods learned. For example, TIY teachers are commonly taught to perform the physical poses they're teaching along with their students. In some criminal justice contexts, however, it may be critical that a teacher is able to observe students individually and collectively at all times. In such cases, context-appropriate methods should be prioritized.

Specialized Trainings. DOC administrators ought to be aware that specialized trainings exist for yoga teachers who wish to work with particular populations such as children, youth, seniors, veterans, pregnancy, and people with unique physical and mental health challenges such as traumatic brain injury and recovery from addiction. If yoga is being offered to some such particular group(s), teachers should be required to have appropriate specialized training or equivalent professional background experience before beginning to teach.

More generally, yoga teachers are advised to pursue specialized training that will equip them to work knowledgeably with conditions of poor health and physical limitation common among system-involved people. Recommended trainings include but are not limited to "chair yoga" (for students with balance issues, spinal or other injuries, and/or difficulty moving down to and up from the floor) and "larger-bodied" or "curvy" yoga (for students of bigger size).

Selecting Trainings. The geographic availability of 200-hour, trauma-informed, and specialized trainings varies tremendously. Major urban areas are more likely to have good options available. Even there, though, they will only be up and running at certain times. Many yoga studios offer 200-hour trainings. Their quality, however, varies significantly.

The protracted time commitment and substantial costs involved in taking a 200-hour YTT, which often cost around $3,000, are difficult or prohibitive for some people. Prospective teachers may be able to defray costs by obtaining scholarships, either from the YTT provider itself or a specialized program. The Yoga Alliance Foundation, for example, offers scholarships to YA-registered YTT programs; the Kripalu Center for Yoga and Health offers them for its 200-hour YTT program.

Because 200-hour YTTs provide the foundation for yoga teaching and require so much time, they demand to be done in person. Short, specialized trainings, however, may in some cases be appropriate to do online. As a general rule, in-person training is preferable. That said, good online trainings are increasingly available and may sometimes be the best option.

In all cases, yoga service organizations and individual teachers should carefully research the best options available in their areas. Generally speaking, this requires spending time researching online options, talking with knowledgeable sources, and studying any yoga-themed print publications that may exist locally. In cases where no such source is known, contacting local studios and asking for help in locating anyone with experience teaching yoga in the criminal justice system may be helpful.

As discussed previously, yoga service organizations should prioritize developing their own specialized training as their knowledge and capacity grows and allows.

"I feel that with the right trauma-informed and evidence-based approach, the justice system is willing to adopt changes that can better the environment for all involved. As yoga service providers, we can offer many opportunities for transformation—transformation within this system and society as a whole. This shift must begin deep within each one of us."[7]

TRAINING AND STAFFING: REQUIRE PROFICIENCY IN TRAUMA-INFORMED YOGA

Yoga teachers should understand the theory and practice of trauma-informed yoga, and be capable of teaching it effectively.

Trauma-informed yoga training should be a strict requirement for teachers working in the criminal justice system. Simply having such training, however, doesn't necessarily create proficiency. As much as possible, individual teachers should assess their understanding of TIY theory and practice, and seek additional study and guidance as necessary to have a solid foundation to build on before beginning to teach. Yoga service organizations should also screen and assess their teachers to ensure that they are able to teach TIY effectively.

Simply learning a set of impersonal tools and methods is not enough. Working with people who have experienced trauma in sensitive, supportive, and healing ways requires maturity, self-knowledge, and the capacity to maintain healthy boundaries and relationships. As discussed in chapter 4, "Relationship Building,"

---

7   All highlighted quotes in this book are provided by contributors and listed without attribution
     in keeping with the collaborative structure of the work as a whole.

this requires ongoing work of self-care, self-reflection, and self-inquiry on the part of the teacher, as well as the capacity to connect this internal work to the practice of what the Yoga Service Council calls "conscious relationship" (Childress & Cohen Harper, 2016).

As part of this process, it is critical that TIY teachers investigate and work through whatever personal history of trauma they may have. The relationship between having experienced trauma and being able to teach TIY can be complex. For example, teachers who suffered childhood abuse and are not yet sufficiently healed from it may have a sincere desire to serve coupled with an unconscious need to be in a position of power and have control over students. Such cravings for undue authority can serve as an unhealthy substitute for the sense of personal power that was stolen from them by their abusers. If such dynamics seem to be occurring, it's crucial that teachers stop teaching until their own issues have been more thoroughly processed and healthy teacher-student relationships can be fostered and maintained.

Yoga service organizations should actively support ongoing learning and professional development among their teaching staff. When possible, offering in-house TIY trainings that are geared toward the specific institutional setting and population being served is ideal. As their capacity grows, yoga service organizations may consider expanding to offer TIY trainings to correctional and administrative staff.

Understanding Trauma. Trauma occurs when people experience "inescapable shock": real or perceived threats to physical survival and/or psychoemotional integrity experienced in circumstances that prevent safe escape and/or overwhelm the capacity to cope. Traumatic experiences activate our instinctual fight-flight-freeze response, a powerful impetus to fight back, run away, or freeze up in the face of danger. This response pattern is hardwired into the human nervous system to help us protect ourselves from serious harm. Trauma occurs when this self-protective response proves insufficient and we are unable to escape a physically threatening and/or psychologically overwhelming situation (Horton et al., 2016).

Trauma-informed yoga is based on the understanding that trauma adversely impacts the mind-body system as a whole. As such, the physiological and psychological effects of trauma are inextricable. As trauma expert Dr. Bessel van der Kolk explains: "Trauma is not just an event that took place sometime in the past; it is also the imprint left by that experience on mind, brain, and body" (van der Kolk, 2014, p. 21).

If people who have experienced trauma are unable to process and release this shock to their mind-body system, they may remain in a state of severe physiological and psychoemotional disequilibrium. Often, this manifests as hyper- or hypoarousal. People may become stuck in a hypervigilant state of "high alert" regardless of actual circumstance, acutely anxious and obsessively scanning the environment for potential threats. Conversely, they may experience disassociation or feeling "shut down," becoming mired in feelings of lethargy, apathy, depression, and numbing disconnection from life (Horton et al., 2016).

Clinically, such symptoms are associated with a diagnosis of post-traumatic stress disorder, or PTSD. Common PTSD symptoms include having dreams and images of the trauma, experiencing distress at reminders of it, sleep difficulties, problems concentrating, hypervigilance, outbursts of anger, and avoidance of whatever feels associated with the trauma (Whitten, 2012). Such chronic disequilibrium commonly produces or exacerbates additional problems such as substance abuse, disrupted relationships, and major overreactions to minor events. Over the long term, unaddressed PTSD may cause other serious health problems, including cardiovascular disease and diabetes (Horton et al., 2016).

Benefits of Yoga. Trauma-informed yoga is designed to help ease the chronic nervous system activation produced by unprocessed trauma. For those unfamiliar with it (and perhaps with yoga more generally), it is important to realize that TIY represents a relatively distinct way of understanding, teaching, and practicing yoga. While many elements of a trauma-informed yoga class might seem similar to that of a "regular" one (to the extent such an entity exists—there are many varieties of yoga instruction available), others would likely be quite different. In fact, many practices common to mainstream yoga classes contradict trauma-informed methods.

Yoga instruction that is not trauma-informed runs the risk of being triggering or otherwise harmful to students who have experienced trauma. (This is not to claim that TIY will never be triggering; such assurances cannot be made. Trauma-informed methods are, however, designed to minimize this possibility while maximizing the healing potential of yoga for trauma.) For example, it's common for teachers in standard yoga classes to direct students to assume physically and/ or psychologically challenging postures. A trauma-informed teacher, in contrast, would invite them to explore positions and movements selected to maintain a strong sense of personal safety, choice, and control.

While such differences may seem subtle, they are significant. Given that trauma involves physical and/or psychological overwhelm and loss of personal safety, choice, and control, the practice of getting in touch with how one is feeling internally from moment to moment—and responding to that in ways that promote self-regulation or equilibrium and ease in the mind-body system—can be deeply healing. Being told what to do and feeling obligated to perform regardless of how it may feel physically or emotionally, in contrast, may be triggering or otherwise problematic. (For a detailed discussion of recommended TIY methods in a criminal justice context, see chapter 3, "Curriculum and Instruction.")

Correlation with Incarceration. Traumatic events may be one-time occurrences, such as a car crash, or part of an ongoing pattern, such as child abuse or neglect. Traumatic experiences that are multiple and ongoing may create a condition known as "complex trauma." People who have experienced complex trauma are at exceptionally high risk for a variety of physical and mental illnesses, substance abuse and addiction problems, and challenges with healthy interpersonal relationships and pro-social behavior (NCTSN, 2017). Traumatic experiences in early childhood carry increased risk of developing complex trauma, which carries with it profound social, emotional, cognitive, and physical implications.[8]

The experience of complex trauma is highly correlated with criminal justice system involvement. One National Institute of Justice study conducted in 2001 found that being abused or neglected as a child increased the likelihood of arrest as a youth by 59 percent. Abuse and neglect also increased the likelihood of adult criminal behavior by 28 percent and violent crime by 30 percent (CDC, 2016).

The correlation between complex trauma and incarceration is particularly high for women and girls. One study found an estimated 77 to 90 percent of women with drug dependency in prison had extensive histories of emotional, physical, and sexual abuse (Whitten, 2012). Another revealed that 42 percent of system-involved girls reported past physical abuse, compared to 22 percent of boys. Findings of past sexual abuse showed an even greater gender discrepancy, with 35 percent of girls and 8 percent of boys reporting (Epstein & Gonzáles, 2017).

Being incarcerated often exacerbates existing traumas while introducing new ones. As Haney (2001) notes, "the fact that a high percentage of persons presently incarcerated have experienced childhood trauma means, among other things, that the harsh, punitive, and uncaring nature of prison life may represent a kind of 're-traumatization' experience for many of them" (para. 32).

Working in a correctional facility also tends to be extremely stressful and, at times, traumatic. Research indicates that correctional officers have 39 percent higher suicide rates than people in other professions, as well as reduced life expectancy linked to stress-related conditions such as high blood pressure, heart attacks, and ulcers (Lopez, 2014).

Undiagnosed Trauma. In many cases, incarcerated persons and correctional officers have never been diagnosed with trauma and have little or no understanding

---

8   The foundational research on the impact of childhood trauma is the CDC-Kaiser Adverse Childhood Experiences (ACE) study. For information on this and related work and its significance and utilization, see https://www.cdc.gov/violenceprevention/acestudy/index.html.

of their own trauma-related symptoms and behaviors. It's important for yoga teachers to be aware that trauma may be present even in the absence of a diagnosis. They should understand that people may be uncomfortable discussing their experiences of trauma or even find such a suggestion insulting.

Yoga teachers should remain strictly within the boundaries of their own profession and refrain from any independent assessments of their students or anyone else with regard to trauma. Instead, teachers are encouraged to continue to deepen their understanding of the theory and practice of trauma-informed yoga through ongoing study and experience.

Mandatory vs. Voluntary Programs How different individuals respond to yoga can and does vary enormously. And, like any therapeutic intervention, trauma-informed yoga is only effective when people have or develop the internal motivation to engage with it meaningfully.

The fact that internal motivation is so vital to yoga raises the question of whether classes in the criminal justice system should always be voluntary or whether mandatory participation can be beneficial as well. Currently, there is no research-based data to draw on to help answer this question. Contributors to this book have varied opinions on whether mandated participation in yoga classes may be appropriate—and if so, for which populations and under what sort of conditions.

- **Youth.** Considerations concerning mandated programming vary significantly between youth and adults, as incarcerated youth are usually placed in some sort of mandated educational curriculum. Integrating yoga into established curricula is recommended provided that trauma-informed principles remain intact. This means that even if youth are required to attend a yoga class as part of their educational programming, they are still able to choose whether to participate actively in the class. For example, choosing to practice the poses taught, take more passive or otherwise modified alternatives, or lie down quietly are equally valid, provided the choice does not negatively impact the experience of others.

Exercising this sort of choice is foundational to TIY and should not be compromised. Experts recognize that simply being in the presence of those practicing yoga can be healing and beneficial. This means that pose modifications, alternatives, and opt-outs may be welcomed as part of the practice unless clearly disruptive.

In some cases, youth are given a choice of different program options, with yoga classes included as part of their mandated choice set. In others, youth are provided with incentives (e.g., school credit, grocery store coupons, certificate of completion) to participate in various program options, of which yoga is one. Contributors who teach yoga to youth under such conditions find that this sort of mandated or incentivized choice works well provided that trauma-informed principles are maintained and the requirement of being nondisruptive to others enforced. They also note that most of these youth almost certainly would not be exposed to yoga without such structured programs and incentives. In their experience, many young people who assume that yoga is not for them quickly discover that they like and benefit from it after all.

- **Adults.** The question of mandated yoga classes for adults is more complex. Some of the contributors to this manual do not favor them under any circumstances, on the grounds that they contradict trauma-informed principles, tend to be ineffective, and risk disrupting the benefits provided by purely voluntary programs. Others believe that mandatory classes can work well provided that: (1) the teacher is aware and supportive, and (2) students are given as much freedom of choice as possible within the class, in keeping with trauma-informed principles. (See chapter 3, "Curriculum and Instruction," for a fuller discussion of this issue.)

If criminal justice professionals are working with or interested in developing mandated programs, it is advisable for them to do so in consultation with experienced yoga service providers. Coordination is needed to make sure that the needs, requirements, capacities, and goals of the system-based mandate and yoga service program align.

Whether voluntary or mandated, yoga service providers and criminal justice professionals alike should remember that trauma-informed yoga is not intended to be a stand-alone therapy. When possible, combining TIY with appropriate complementary interventions (e.g., cognitive behavioral therapy) is recommended. In most cases, the synergy between complementary modalities will make each substantially more effective.

Training Components. All trauma-informed yoga trainings should be research-based. Ideally, they should also include but not be limited to the following elements:

- The debate on how to define psychological trauma and the limitations of such definitions, especially with regard to diagnosis

- The physiological impacts of psychological trauma

- The implications of untreated trauma on the individual

- The impact of early childhood trauma and subsequent domains of impairment as defined by the Adverse Childhood Experiences (ACE) study

- The incidence of individual, intergenerational, systemic, and historic trauma in the general population and in system-involved populations

- The limitations of talk therapy in addressing trauma and the therapeutic value of somatic-based practices, including but not limited to yoga

- The reasons why yoga-based posture and breath work can support self-regulation, positively impact the autonomic and parasympathetic nervous systems, develop proprioceptive and interoceptive skills,[9] and deepen emotional and sensory awareness

---

9   Proprioception is the ability to sense the physical location and movement of your body in and through space. Interoception is being able to sense internal feeling states, including gross and subtle sensations inside the body.

Recommended teaching techniques for trauma-informed yoga classes are discussed in chapter 3, "Curriculum and Instruction." General resources on trauma-informed yoga are listed in Appendix A.

> "Even though instructors may understand on a cognitive level how important it is to offer yoga that's trauma-informed, that's not enough. For most of us, it takes ongoing effort, mentoring, and practice to fully integrate these concepts into our teaching practice."

TRAINING AND STAFFING: PROACTIVELY ADDRESS SECONDARY TRAUMA

Yoga teachers should understand the causes and effects of secondary trauma and work proactively to prevent and address it.

Working in the criminal justice system can be highly stressful and can put people at risk of developing what's commonly referred to as "secondary trauma" (sometimes referred to as "vicarious trauma," "trauma-exposure response," or "compassion fatigue"). A common problem among helping professionals and others who work closely with people who have experienced or are currently experiencing trauma, secondary trauma occurs when "external trauma becomes internal reality." Although symptoms vary widely, common ones include hypervigilance, diminished creativity, avoidance, disassociative moments, hopelessness, chronic exhaustion, inability to listen, fear, guilt, anger, cynicism, and grandiosity (van Dernoot Lipsky, 2009, p. 42).

It's vital that yoga service organizations and individual teachers alike are committed to the proactive management of secondary trauma for both their own well-being and the integrity of their work in the criminal justice system. As individuals and a collective, they need to be familiar with common symptoms of secondary trauma and self-evaluate regularly.

It is important that yoga teachers have a clearly established self-care practice, including but not limited to confidential disclosure and mental and physical self-care practices. They should commit to monitoring their own stress levels regularly and be prepared to manage them proactively.

All teachers should have access to a peer network in which they can safely discuss their experiences in the criminal justice system without breaking confidentiality. Yoga service organizations can facilitate this vital support by building fellowship, post-class discussions, and peer-to-peer sharing into their trainings and operations. (For an in-depth discussion of self- and collective-care practices, see chapter 4, "Relationship Building.")

Support Systems. Yoga service organizations should have a plan for identifying and addressing secondary trauma among staff and teachers. This might include regular check-ins, developing a mentoring or buddy system, referrals to mental health support services, and provision of these services in-house when possible. Organizations that offer yoga teacher trainings should consider developing closed and confidential message groups and other long-distance supports to their graduates, including those not currently working with them.

Access to needed support is difficult for a teacher working independently, and isolation can contribute to stress and burnout. Consequently, teachers who anticipate or are working alone are encouraged connect with providers who offer long-distance support, if possible.

Resilience. Resiliency is the ability to recover equilibrium after being exposed to stressful situations. As such, it is a valuable quality to cultivate both in and of itself, and as a means of reducing risk of secondary trauma.

Yoga service providers should consider how to build individual and organizational resilience, and emphasize resiliency building in self-care practices, yoga teacher trainings, teacher support strategies, and staff and leadership development. Leaders of yoga service organizations may similarly wish to consider seeking out leaders of other groups doing similar work who might be interested in developing a relationship that offers mutual understanding and support.

"We found at times, even after our decompression chat—which we called 'powwows'—that we would call another teacher driving home from teaching yoga in juvenile hall. Sometimes there were tears, shared joy, and memories that came up from our own youth that were triggered and needed to be shared with another yoga teacher."

"Something we have found helpful to help with secondary trauma is co-teaching and scheduling program-wide breaks. We recently instated a month-long summer break for the majority of our programs. Many of our instructors are so dedicated to their students that they feel bad for leaving them without yoga for even a week. This organization-mandated break gives our instructors permission to take some important time away."

TRAINING AND STAFFING:
KNOW AND FOLLOW SAFETY AND
SECURITY PROCEDURES

Yoga teachers must understand the safety and security rules and procedures of the institution they're working in, and follow them strictly and without exception.

The possibility of serious conflict or violent conduct is always a concern when working with a court-involved population. This is a sensitive topic, raising valid concerns about the risk of stereotyping and prejudicial expectations. Yoga teachers may have more positive beliefs about an individual's capacity to act consistently from their better nature than criminal justice professionals and staff. However, they must understand and respect the fact that correctional officers are mandated to ensure safety in facilities at all times.

Regardless of the actual level of risk, all yoga service organizations and individual teachers should understand and follow the safety and security rules and procedures presented in correctional systems trainings, orientations, and conduct requirements at all times. *Facility regulations MUST supersede all other concerns or directives.* Failure to comply with them puts students, teachers, and correctional staff at increased risk, jeopardizes the continuation of the yoga program, and discredits the project of offering yoga in the criminal justice system as a whole.

> "The facility has both the authority and responsibility to deny access to any person whose presence is believed to jeopardize order, security or safety within it."

It is imperative that yoga teachers work collaboratively and respectfully with facility partners and other criminal justice staff. Yoga service providers should understand and respect the distinct roles of facility staff and yoga teachers, and prioritize developing positive channels of communication. Yoga teachers must give facility staff every indication that they are committed to safety and security concerns and priorities. Some important guidelines include:

- If a DOC-sponsored safety and security training is available, complete it before beginning to teach.

- More well-established yoga service organizations might explore the possibility of collaborating with a facility or court-ordered program to add a yoga-specific component into their established training or to develop a dedicated training for yoga teachers and staff.

- If a facility does not require that a correctional officer be present during classes, the teacher or organization should inquire whether it's possible. Some institutions do not have sufficient staff to cover all program activities. If staff cannot be present, request that the class be held in a room with security cameras. As these are closely monitored, they offer a workable substitute. Leaving a teacher unaccompanied and/ or unobservable during class or while traversing a facility should be considered with utmost care for both their own safety and that of their students and the facility staff.

- Yoga teachers should understand the chain of command within a facility from the initial contact person to the program supervisor, and how to report any problematic incidents properly.

- Those working with a yoga service organization additionally need to know and follow their own internal reporting requirements and procedures, and communicate issues fully to leaders and staff.

- Yoga teachers must defer to probation/custodial staff during an emergency (typically referred to as "lockdowns" or "codes"). Rather than initiating a response, they should wait to follow directions issued by facility staff.

- Yoga teachers need to ask facility or program staff before doing anything out of the ordinary such as giving the students something or taking them somewhere other than the practice space. They should never initiate independent actions that have not had prior approval.

- Yoga teachers should never: (1) accept anything from a student to deliver to someone else such as a note or a gift; (2) let a student leave the room or use the bathroom without staff approval; or (3) exchange personal information with students. They should receive training on appropriate boundaries, including maintaining confidentiality and nondisclosure.

- When possible, yoga teachers ought to avoid telling students their full names. (Post-release programs, in which students transitioning out of the system continue working with teachers in the community, are an exception to this general rule.)

- Yoga service providers must know what is considered contraband in the facility and be compliant with all applicable rules. Contraband may include seemingly benign items such as cardigans, hairpins, keys, CDs, paper (particularly but not exclusively if stapled), and yoga props. Teachers should always request permission before bringing in new teaching materials or resources.

> "One of our most dedicated and long-time instructors got stuck inside a facility during a safety lockdown. The instructor was upset because he was missing an appointment and challenged the prison staff to let him leave. He was promptly suspended and no longer allowed to teach."

Safety and Security Trainings. Most correctional facilities require completion of some form of orientation training prior to admittance. In many cases, this training is required on an annual basis. The scope and scale of these trainings vary greatly from state to state and facility to facility. Training may include a brief review of facility conduct requirements (dress code, security procedures, etc.) or incorporate additional components such as the Prison Rape Elimination Act (PREA), which provides guidance on practices designed to eliminate sexual assault and harassment behind bars.

Even if a facility provides good training, yoga service organizations should consider how it might be supplemented and reinforced. In cases where a facility offers minimal or no training, they should develop the capacity to offer the best possible equivalent in-house. Individuals who are teaching yoga in the criminal justice system independently, rather than as part of an organization, are advised to seek clarification of facility policies regarding emergency procedures, reporting of incidents, and other facility regulations from their authorizing contact person. They should also find a way to access PREA training if possible, or at least review relevant materials online.

Yoga service providers should be trained in CPR and have a clear understanding of what the facility safety procedure is, should anyone require it. CPR training is frequently available through local hospitals as well as through fire and rescue services. The American Red Cross offers low-cost CPR training for certification as well as on-line training for those who wish to learn the skills but don't need to be certified.

When possible, yoga service training should include conflict management and verbal de-escalation. While an in-depth training may not be possible for small volunteer-based organizations or individual teachers, there are multiple free resources available online. Although untrained teachers should not practice specific de-escalation techniques, familiarity with the general approach can be helpful.

Background Checks. Each individual teacher needs to have a background check completed. Often, facilities offer to handle this procedure. If this is not the case, yoga service organizations or individual teachers must contract with an agency to complete this service and budget accordingly. The average per-person cost is about $75.

Having a criminal record does not necessarily prohibit a prospective teacher from working behind bars. However, it is critical that any record is disclosed upfront.

Reporting Requirements. Yoga teachers working as volunteers or contractors in prisons, jails, or other detention facilities may have reporting requirements regarding situations and behavior they witness or are told about. For example, most facilities require reporting statements or behaviors that might indicate someone is contemplating or planning a suicide attempt. Teachers should know what the chain of command is for reporting incidents and other problems within both the facility and the yoga service organization.

Any yoga service organization that works with young people in youth justice settings should require their teachers to attend a Mandated Reporter training before beginning to work. Mandated Reporter trainings support state and/or federal statutes that require professionals who typically have frequent contact with children (e.g., social workers, school teachers, childcare providers, health care workers) to report any suspected child abuse or maltreatment they encounter (CWIF, 2015). Reporting requirements are complex, and yoga teachers will not be able to understand and comply with them properly without training.

The Prison Rape Elimination Action (PREA) requires institutions to provide training to staff and volunteers on how to prevent, detect, and respond to sexual violence in federal, state, and local institutions. Yoga teachers should understand reporting procedures if sexual harassment or violence is suspected, witnessed, or reported directly to the teacher. (The PREA statute requires action to be taken if yoga instructors are told about an incident, even if they did not witness it themselves.)

Teachers may be required to track students' participation and progress for official reasons. They should understand that reporting disruptive or inappropriate behavior is a serious matter. It is necessary to maintain the safety and security of the facility for all. It is also likely to have consequences for individual students, and demand substantial staff time and energy. When in doubt about what to report, teachers should confer with their organizational leader, if they have one, or another trusted and knowledgeable source.

If teachers have problems with facility staff, they are advised to report incidents to their yoga service organization, if they are part of one. Each organization should develop clear procedures and a chain of command for handling such incidents. Individual teachers should never be confrontational with staff, and avoid handling problems with them directly, if possible.

TRAINING AND STAFFING: UNDERSTAND ISSUES OF GENDER AND SEXUALITY

Training programs must sufficiently inform and educate yoga teachers regarding issues of gender and gender identity, and sexual identity and orientation.

Yoga teachers working in the criminal justice system should be trained on issues related to sexual orientation and gender identity, and comfortable working with people of all varieties of gender expression. Gender sensitivity training should include but not be limited to: (1) the difference between gender, gender identity, and sexual orientation; (2) common misconceptions about gender and sexuality; (3) relevant historical and contemporary power differentials; and (4) gender-spectrum supportive language and behavioral tools.

Correctional facilities are gender binary, with separate male and female facilities. Trainings should include, and individual teachers should consider, the potential impact of gender segregation on an incarcerated population, particularly when staffed solely or predominantly by people of the same gender.

States differ on how to classify transgender people. It is more common to incarcerate an individual according to observed biological traits at birth than to consider gender identity. Non-cisgender individuals are frequently held in isolation and may be at a significantly higher risk of violence and abuse, particularly in male facilities.

Yoga classes may be one of the few safe spaces for individuals who do not conform to the gender binary. Gender-reflective language and acceptance of all bodies should be part of all yoga programming.

Sexual Orientation. Sexuality is a universal and powerful driving force that informs many of our social interactions. Although sexuality may not be a direct part of yoga classes, understanding of and respect for this primal drive is important.

It's important for yoga teachers to be aware that:

- Sexual activity between two or more people is prohibited in correctional facilities, as the state of incarceration is believed to render consent impossible.

- Sexual activity occurs in correctional facilities nonetheless, both as an expression of intimacy and as an act of power and domination.

- Sensitivity to the clandestine and highly charged nature of sexual attraction is important.

- It is imperative to have self-knowledge regarding one's own sensitivities and potential triggers on gender and sexuality issues, as well as resources for self-regulation and self-management, should they arise.

- It's important to be prepared to address and manage overt expressions of sexuality or sexual behavior, which may occur unexpectedly during or while in transit to class. Teachers should not remain passive and simply hope that problematic behaviors dissipate on their own. Instead, they're encouraged to take calm, measured, assertive action to maintain appropriate boundaries (e.g., politely but firmly tell a student that he or she must respect your personal space in order to continue participating in class).

Gender Responsiveness. The majority of therapeutic programs offered in correctional facilities have been based on research conducted with men. Stephanie

Covington, PhD, offers compelling research that indicates that these approaches are not necessarily beneficial for girls and women behind bars, and may indeed be harmful. Her work provides the most widely recognized guidelines for gender-appropriate programming for both men and women in prisons.[10]

It is important that yoga teachers receive training in relevant gender-responsive issues, including but not limited to gender differences in response to trauma and stress. Although the term "gender responsive" is generally used to designate practices appropriate for girls and women, gender-sensitive yoga should consider the needs of all gender identities.

Women and Girls. Although they remain a significant minority, women and girls make up the fastest-growing component of the incarcerated population, with an increase in numbers far outpacing that of men's during the past 40 years. Although there is limited research data on incarcerated women, a 2016 report by the Vera Institute of Justice cites that the vast majority of these women are held in local and county jails, in most cases for nonviolent offences (Swavola, Riley, & Subramanian, 2016).

Women and girls behind bars present a unique set of complex needs that are often overlooked by a predominantly male system. Eighty percent of women in jail are mothers, most of them single parents. Eighty-six percent report experiencing physical and/or sexual assault prior to incarceration. The rate of serious mental illness among this group is 32 percent, more than double that of men in jail. Common practices in incarceration can significantly increase the impact of previous trauma and can lead to great risk of triggering or exacerbating further mental illness (Swavola, Riley, & Subramanian, 2016).

---

10 The most up-to-date information on Dr. Covington's work can be found on her website, http://www.stephaniecovington.com.

TRAINING AND STAFFING:
EXERCISE MAXIMAL AWARENESS
AND FULL PRESENCE

Yoga teachers should be trained to maximize their power of awareness and to be fully present at all times in correctional facilities.

Teaching in correctional facilities demands maintaining a consistently high level of awareness and presence. This includes but is by no means limited to the context of the yoga class itself. Professional attention and self-awareness should be held from the parking lot, in and out of the facility, and back to the parking lot (or bus stop, etc.). Being fully aware and present includes exercising maximal capacities of seeing, listening, hearing, verbalizing, sensing, and moment-to-moment responding.

Good trauma-informed yoga trainings should help teachers develop this level of personal sensitivity and awareness. Good prison-focused yoga trainings should provide clear examples of how to apply this level of awareness to the role of teaching in a corrections setting.

Yoga service organizations are advised to prioritize ensuring that teachers understand the importance of maintaining full awareness and presence in their work, as well as concrete tools for doing so. Well-trained yoga teachers have a well-developed capacity to self-monitor and assess whether they are alert or distracted. They understand how to work with their own breath regulation and sensory capacities to remain maximally present, aware, centered, calm, and grounded, and strive to do so as much as possible.

Solo teachers working without the support of a yoga service organization are encouraged to seek relevant training and pursue independent study and practice to meet this best practice guideline.

TRAINING AND STAFFING: FOLLOW PROFESSIONAL CODES AND ETHICAL GUIDELINES

Teachers should strictly follow codes of conduct and ethical guidelines provided by yoga trainings, professional governing bodies, and correctional facilities.

Although yoga is an unregulated field, professional codes of conduct, as well as ethical and scope of practice guidelines, are provided by major professional associations including Yoga Alliance and the International Association of Yoga Therapists.[11] Yoga teacher trainings and/or yoga service organizations may have additional guidelines of their own. Where available, all yoga teachers and service organization staff *must* comply with all relevant facility codes of conduct and ethical guidelines.

Yoga service providers should understand that while following professional codes of conduct and ethical guidelines is always important, it is particularly critical in the criminal justice system. Service organizations and individual teachers should recognize that the conduct of one person or group has the potential to impact the reputation of yoga in the criminal justice arena broadly.

Confidentiality and Consent. Yoga service providers should be aware that court involvement has significant immediate and long-term implications for individuals that can affect such major domains of life as education, employment, housing, and personal relationships. Being incarcerated is understood to significantly diminish or render null an individual's capacity for informed consent. While it is critical to respect the agency of all people, free or incarcerated, it is also necessary to recognize that system-involved people are particularly vulnerable to potential exploitation and that confidentiality issues are paramount.

---

11   These guidelines are available online at https://www.yogaalliance.org/YACodeOfConduct and http://www.iayt.org/news/283996/Code-of-Ethics--Scope-of-Practice.htm.

Yoga service organizations and individual teachers who promote their work for fundraising, social justice, or other reasons should do so with a strict regard to the privacy and rights of both system-involved individuals and system staff. They should be aware that correctional officers may live in or come from the same community as the incarcerated populations they are monitoring. For privacy and safety reasons, it is common for facilities to hold the names of staff privately.

Social Media Policy. Yoga service organizations are encouraged to develop a policy on personal and professional social media usage for all staff and volunteers. If yoga trainings are offered, this policy should apply to all trainees and graduates, not only those who teach with the organization.

Social media policies should emphasize the importance of good judgment, common sense, courtesy, and respect for system-involved people, criminal justice professionals, and corrections staff. They should stipulate that yoga teachers, staff, and volunteers refrain from any actions that are or could be deemed unlawful such as harassment or discrimination. Confidentiality of the individuals they have taught, worked with, or encountered in prisons or jails should be strictly maintained.

Full transparency and informed consent should govern any social media postings or other promotional materials that reference or quote a yoga student who is or has been system-involved. For example, if students are asked to provide formal or written feedback on yoga classes, they ought to clearly understand whether quotes might be used publicly for promotional or educational purposes, and have the option to opt out. Whenever possible, yoga service providers should ask if they can share someone's story before doing so. Even when consent is given, changing names for confidentiality purposes is recommended.

Yoga teachers, staff, or volunteers who make personal social media postings about their work should make it clear that they do not represent their yoga service organization. If they are unsure how to do this or whether what they have in mind is otherwise appropriate, they should refrain from posting until they have received guidance from their organization's designated point person (most likely, the executive director).

Yoga service providers need to be aware that facilities prohibit unauthorized photography on their grounds, including outside and in front of buildings. Any pictures taken without permission and posted on social media may result in the offending teacher and organization being barred from future entry.

TRAINING AND STAFFING: ASSESS TEACHER READINESS

Yoga service organizations should have protocols in place to assess the readiness of teachers both before and after hiring.

It's important that yoga service organizations develop and implement an informative but easy-to-use assessment tool to screen potential teachers. Screening questions that organizations may want to consider include but are not limited to: (1) date and provider of core trainings (i.e., 200-hour YTT, TIY training, other specialized trainings); (2) understanding of and proficiency with TIY principles; (3) availability for facility-provided orientation (if applicable); (4) times available to teach; and (5) stated length of commitment to the program.

Having the same individual teach a given class regularly is a vital component of a trauma-informed yoga program. A disproportionately high percentage of the incarcerated population has experienced a history of disruption in their personal relationships and/or living situations. Having a consistent teacher and class plan supports the sense of predictability and safety that makes TIY more effective.

Consequently, yoga service organizations and correctional systems staff should consider how long a prospective teacher is able to reliably dedicate to a given class. Six months of regular attendance should be considered a bare minimum. A year or more is preferable.

To the extent it is organizationally possible and appropriate, the minimum time commitment may be specified in a signed contract, along with other agreed-upon stipulations such as confidentiality, social media policy, liability insurance requirements, and so on.

Ongoing Assessment. As yoga service organizations develop, they should continue to assess teachers on a regular, and at least annual, basis. Recommended issues to consider include but are not limited to: (a) responsiveness to training and feedback, (b) compliance with organizational and facility protocols, and (c) attendance record.

When assessing teachers, it is highly recommended to solicit their feedback on the organization and program as well. Encouraging open lines of communication and providing structured opportunities for feedback creates stronger and more effective organizations.

TRAINING AND STAFFING:
RECRUIT A DIVERSE TEACHING STAFF

Yoga service organizations should seek to recruit a diverse teaching staff that reflects and supports the population being served.

Yoga service organizations should be familiar with the population they are serving and strive to recruit teachers from a similar background or demographic. The power of being inspired by a teacher one can identify with should not be underestimated.

Generally speaking, the demographic profiles of yoga teachers and system-involved people are quite different. In the United States, yoga teachers are disproportionately white, female, and middle to upper income. System-involved people are disproportionately black, Latino, male, and low income. This demographic mismatch means that recruiting an appropriately diverse teaching staff will likely require community outreach and seeking participants from nontraditional yoga settings.

Wherever possible, organizations and individual teachers who do not have personal experience with the criminal justice system should connect with and be informed by those who do. Seeking out and respecting the experiences and wisdom of both those who work in or with the system and those who are or have been system-involved will do much to enhance the appropriateness and applicability of teachings offered.

As the number of yoga programs in correctional facilities expands, there are increasing numbers of returning citizens who have experienced yoga while incarcerated. Yoga service organizations should seek to include such individuals in diversity trainings, speaking engagements, events, and, where appropriate, as teachers. Those with sufficient capacity may also consider creating and/or supporting scholarships for people with a history of incarceration who wish to attend yoga teacher training programs in order to teach yoga.

> "Sometimes we don't 'match' the population we serve. If done appropriately and with boundaries, sharing our 'personal story' with our students can go a long way. Relate and let them know why you are there. Our outer appearance might look one way, but the reality is different. This can be a powerful way to break down barriers."

Implicit Bias. It is important that teachers have an understanding of their own privileges and implicit biases, and that they have received training on these issues. It is critical that yoga organizations realize that they may not be best positioned to train their own staff on these often-challenging matters. If this is the case, they should research and secure a high-quality external provider. Teachers and organizations must understand that they may inadvertently cause harm to their students without proper training and support.

Personal Readiness. Some individuals are drawn to TIY and/or teaching in the criminal justice system because of their own past experiences with trauma, incarceration, or other personal issues. Yoga service organizations should consider supportive training and mentorship for such individuals to ensure readiness, where appropriate. They should retain the right to reject a teaching application or dismiss teachers when necessary. Difficult as this may be, no one is served by teachers meeting their own needs at the expense of the yoga program and its participants.

TRAINING AND STAFFING:
CONSIDER DIVERSIFIED TEACHING TEAMS

Service organizations should consider having yoga teachers work in diversified pairs, if possible.

It's important that teachers be fully present and vigilant about what is happening in their classes. They must keep their eyes on the students and on the environment at all times. To that end and where possible, service organizations should consider partner teachers—one who verbally "leads" the flow of class and sometimes demonstrates postures, and another who "assists" and watches everything, addressing behavioral issues and trauma manifestations that arise.

Ideally, teaching teams should be reflective of the diversity of human experience. This includes but is not limited to diversity of gender, race, ethnicity, body type, body size, ability, and life experience. The power of a positive example of diverse individuals working together to offer a positive, healing, and life-affirming yoga practice should not be underestimated. That said, diversity issues are inherently challenging, and supervision and support in navigating them is of fundamental importance.

When circumstances permit, having a male and female co-teach can serve to model a healthy, equitable, and balanced relationship between the sexes. Due to the high incidence of male-generated sexual violence among system-involved females, however, this is recommended for male facilities only.

TRAINING AND STAFFING: CONSIDER CROSS-GENDER TEACHING CAREFULLY

Service organization trainings must address and individual teachers must consider issues of gender and sexuality when teaching across a gender divide.

Approximately 92 percent of the U.S. prison population is male. More than 80 percent of American yoga teachers are female. Expanding access to trauma-informed, gender-sensitive yoga among the system-involved population correspondingly requires having female teachers work in male facilities. Careful consideration of the gender dynamics this involves is critical.

Criminal justice professionals and yoga service provides should be aware that many hundreds of yoga classes are currently being offered by teachers who don't match the gender of their students in correctional facilities across the United States. In the vast majority of cases, both teachers and students are focused on the shared practice of yoga, and engage with each other with mutual respect.

That said, issues of gender- and sexuality-based power and aggression are well documented. This is a very sensitive topic, raising valid concerns about the risk of stereotyping and prejudicial expectations. Real and imagined behaviors heavily influence all parties involved. It is unrealistic and irresponsible for service organizations and individual teachers to ignore or deny these forces. Concerns about violence are also likely to be high among custody staff whose primary responsibility is to ensure safety.

Service organization trainings should proactively address common fears and assumptions in a realistic and open manner, and be prepared to present accurate, research-based data to challenge misconceptions. Trainings should include the fact that much gender-based and sexual violence occurs when the intended victim is understood to be powerless or socially constrained in their response. Service organizations and individual teachers are encouraged to emphasize the validity of "gut responses" to perceived inappropriate action or threat, as well as reinforce the importance of speaking out and acting in a self-protective manner.

Given the high rate of physical and sexual violence that many girls and women have experienced from members of the opposite sex, as well as cultural norms of gender inequity, it is challenging for a male teacher to create a sense of a secure and safe space for girls or women in a correctional facility. Consequently, unless there are compelling reasons to the contrary, it is recommended that men do not teach in female facilities.

TRAINING AND STAFFING:
CONSIDER TRAINING IN DATA COLLECTION AND PROGRAM EVALUATION

As discussed in chapter 5, "Organizational Development," yoga service organizations should set up basic data-collection protocols so that they can document and evaluate their program systematically. To facilitate and support this process, they should, if possible, develop trainings in appropriate data-collection methods for teachers and staff so that there is shared knowledge about why it is important and how to do it responsibly.

Collecting and analyzing program information on a regular basis is important for several reasons: It enables teachers, programs, and organizations to improve by identifying their strengths and weaknesses along with opportunities and challenges. Having solid program data is critical when it comes to seeking funding or pursuing contracts, as most grant makers and potential clients will want solid information on what the program does and how well it is working before supporting it. Program documentation and evaluation is also important for the growth and development of the yoga service field as a whole. Without it, there is no way of sharing and building knowledge systematically.

Yoga service organizations should clear any data collection procedures with appropriate DOC contacts before implementing them. Any opportunities for cooperative data collection and sharing should be explored and discussed. In all cases, it is critical to maintain confidentiality around any personal information concerning students or teachers. Data should be anonymous unless consent has been obtained to share information such as written statements on program benefits and quality. Again, given the importance of these issues, developing or accessing appropriate training for all teachers and staff is recommended.

3

CURRICULUM AND INSTRUCTION

The guiding principle for yoga curriculum and instruction best practices is simple: General trauma-informed yoga methods should be informed by and adapted to the particularities of the criminal justice system. A high incidence of trauma can be assumed present in any class. Given that system-involved people are disproportionately low income and of color, this trauma is likely to be not only personal and familial but also systemic and historic. Being responsive to the individual and collective trauma present in the room, while remaining grounded in one's own personal and social experience, is a precondition for effective trauma-informed yoga (TIY) instruction in any criminal justice context.

As discussed in the preceding chapter, yoga instructors should be trained in trauma-informed yoga prior to beginning to teach. If a teacher is working with a yoga service organization, this training should ideally be provided by them and tailored to the specific facility or program being served. However, relatively few organizations have this capacity. (For a discussion of how it might be developed, see chapter 5, "Organizational Development." For a typology of different stages of organizational development, see Appendix B.) In such cases, it's best to take a TIY training geared toward teaching in a criminal justice context more generally, if possible.

The following discussion is intended to supplement such foundational trauma-informed yoga training. It cannot substitute for it. Accordingly, this chapter does not discuss the general theory and method of TIY in any detail. Instead, it shares principles, information, and insights that are particularly relevant to teaching it in the criminal justice system, focusing on correctional facilities in particular. (For additional resources on TIY, see Appendix A.)

CURRICULUM AND INSTRUCTION: EXPECT A CHALLENGING TEACHING ENVIRONMENT

Yoga teachers should be prepared to teach in conditions significantly more challenging than those of the standard studio or gym class.

Teaching in a correctional facility poses challenges that seldom occur in yoga studios or gyms. Teachers need to understand the nature of these challenges and be personally and professionally equipped to meet them in ways that enhance rather than undermine the yoga practices that they are there to share.

> "How we respond to interruption is a great way to show how the [yoga] practice shows up in real life. Every moment is a teachable moment to show the practice . . . in practice."

Classes may be held in a multipurpose room that has equipment or furniture that must be moved before and after class. They may be held in a large, noisy gym that has different activities going on concurrently. Rooms may need to be cleaned to feel sufficiently inviting to sit down on a mat on the floor. The temperature may be too hot or too cold. There may be extraneous noises that are distracting or disruptive.

Classes may be delayed, interrupted, or canceled with little or no notice. Students may be delayed, blocked, or removed from class. Access to yoga mats, blocks, and other teaching-related equipment may be erratic. Cleaning and storage of equipment may be challenging.

Model Equanimity. It's important that yoga service providers be aware that it is a privilege for a civilian to be permitted entry into a facility, and respond to challenges accordingly. Teachers are advised to maintain a calm and respectful demeanor, modeling equanimity and nonjudgment regardless of whatever disturbances arise.

Facility requirements—including unexpected class cancellations, interruptions, or relocation—supersede all other factors and must be complied with fully. If concerns or disagreements between a teacher and correctional staff develop, they should be resolved through the appropriate channels and not in the moment. Yoga teachers should be aware that if a facility lockdown occurs, they may be unable to leave the facility on time.

Transition Rituals. Many yoga teachers working in challenging environments find it helpful to establish simple personal rituals to support a clean transition out of the teaching role and environment, for example: washing hands, changing clothes, journaling, meditating, or practicing a short *asana* (yoga postures) or *pranayama* (yoga breathing) sequence.

CURRICULUM AND INSTRUCTION: DRESS APPROPRIATELY

Teachers should present themselves in alignment with facility dress codes and with safety in mind.

Suitable clothing for teaching yoga in a correctional facility includes loose-fitting short- or long-sleeved shirts, loose-fitting pants, and shoes that cover the entire foot. Clothes or shoes that might set off a metal detector (e.g., belt buckle, underwire bra, shoes with metal shanks) should be avoided.

Tight and/or revealing clothing, makeup, and perfume may distract from the goals of the practice and may violate system regulations. Teachers should not wear jewelry other than watches, provided they are permitted. Expensive or branded clothing may serve to highlight differences between teacher and students, and should therefore be avoided.

Teachers must avoid wearing colors that students and correctional officers are wearing. They should seek to learn local gang colors and avoid them. Many facilities have rules regarding what colors can be worn, as this makes it easier to distinguish who is and isn't staff in emergency situations. If such rules exist, teachers should follow them precisely.

Teachers should avoid wearing clothing with any text or logos that may disclose extraneous information about themselves such as which university they attended. If service organizations have logos or branded clothing, they should establish clear policies concerning their use in facilities. For personal safety reasons, teachers should refrain from wearing clothing that identifies any other yoga studio or gym where they teach.

CURRICULUM AND INSTRUCTION: CONSIDER ROOM SETUP CAREFULLY

Yoga teachers should carefully consider how to set up the room to maximize student safety, comfort, and privacy.

Careful thinking about how best to configure the space in which yoga classes are held to maximize students' sense of safety, autonomy, and privacy is essential. In so doing, teachers should consider the particularities of their students as much as possible, including their familiarity and relationships with each other.

Mat Configuration. Predictably is a core component of an effective trauma-informed yoga class. Both the teacher's and the students' positions in the room should be predictable. Teachers are wise to carefully consider what sort of mat configuration promises to work best for each particular situation. Once established, it is best not to change it unless there is a compelling reason.

Teachers should be mindful that underlying social dynamics may be impacting why people are in the room and how they choose to position themselves. Within facilities, challenging relationship dynamics can exist between individual students, among groups of incarcerated people, and between them and custody staff. As much as possible, teachers should be sensitive to and respectful of student choices about where they feel most comfortable. There may be reasons behind these decisions that teachers are not privy to.

Some experienced teachers feel that the best configuration is a half circle (horseshoe) or circle, as it removes hierarchy and creates a sense of community. These arrangements follow the trauma-informed principle of not having individuals situated behind one another, which can undermine feelings of security, privacy, and well-being.

Other experts, however, feel that putting mats in rows is a viable option. With this setup, the teacher provides a common focal point. Some teachers believe that students are not as easily triggered by each other in this arrangement as they might be in a circle.

If rows are used, it is helpful for teachers to be sensitive to student dynamics, particularly regarding who is positioned in the back row. In many cases, students feel safest in the back row, as there is nobody behind them. Some, however, many feel better positioned closer to the teacher. Ideally, teachers can help students place themselves in spots that maximize their sense of safety and contribute to positive class dynamics overall.

There is widespread agreement that it's best to place students so that they are facing exits and entrances instead of having their backs to them, if possible. Having the teacher positioned in front of the main door provides more control over ingress and egress, and enables students to see who is coming in and out of the room. As such, this setup is believed to support a greater sense of security and predictability, which is vital to effective TIY instruction.

> "Unfortunately, we can never guarantee complete safety—not inside a prison or jail or outside it. What we can do is create space for people to have the experience of using their breath, their movement, and their mindfulness to better handle the immense challenges of living. What we can do is create a space for brave self-reflection and moments of peace."

Yoga Props. Yoga teachers should never use straps (a commonly used yoga prop) or the equivalent in class. Most facilities follow strict suicide precautions, and straps are an unacceptable risk. Even if permitted by the facility, straps are not recommended, for both this reason and because they could be triggering to students who have experienced being bound against their will.

Some facilities may allow the use of foam blocks (another commonly used yoga prop). Teachers should keep in mind, however, that these and other props may be difficult to store securely and access reliably. Instructors should always be prepared to teach without props if necessary, including without mats. Teachers are encouraged to be creative and resourceful in utilizing whatever natural props are available such as chairs and walls.

Extraneous Items. Teachers should never bring into the facility scissors, sharpeners, or anything that could potentially be used by students to harm themselves or others. Teachers should never use them while inside for any reason. If pens or pencils are utilized, teachers must keep a careful count and alert staff if one is missing. Any handouts that are brought to class must have prior authorization from the facility. For safety reasons, they should never contain staples or paper clips. Multiple-page handouts can be printed to fold together into a booklet that can remain collated without staples.

> "When I first started teaching, the facility had us hold onto the keys of our lockers where we kept our stuff. I misplaced mine, and the facility went on lockdown. Every bed was turned over and every kid was searched until that key was found. The same could be true for a missing hairpin, identification badge, or the cap to a pen. It's important to keep all small loose items inside your pockets."

Student Privacy. There is an inherent "audience" in facilities due to ongoing supervision and the general flow of institutional business. Individuals who students may or may not know can come in and out of the room without warning. In some instances, they may unexpectedly stay to observe the class. When this happens, teachers should avoid instructing students to practice postures that are more likely to make them feel physically or emotionally vulnerable such as Downward-Facing Dog.

Teacher Visibility. The need to respect student privacy must be balanced with the need for teachers to keep a careful eye on their class at all times. This is critical in order to teach effectively, as instruction ought to match students' needs and capacities to the greatest extent possible. As discussed below, teachers must stay alert for signs of increased dysregulation, which could indicate that a student has been triggered during the course of the class, and they should know how to adjust instruction accordingly.

Having teachers "practice with" their students is a standard best practice in trauma-informed yoga. Some poses, however, such as Downward-Facing Dog, prevent clear observation of the class. Although such poses may still be taught, doing so requires breaking the "practice with" rule insofar as doing the posture restricts a teacher's line of sight. Instead, it's recommended that teachers verbally instruct the pose while explaining that they'll be performing a modified version so that they can see what's happening in the class. It is helpful for teachers to word this in terms of being able to see if students are doing a pose safely or may need pointers, rather than communicating some sort of surveillance of them.

CURRICULUM AND INSTRUCTION: DEVELOP YOUTH-SPECIFIC PROTOCOLS

Teachers working with youth must understand youth-specific issues and adapt curriculum and instruction accordingly.

In any context, teaching youth is not the same as teaching adults. Yoga teachers working in the youth justice system should have specialized training in teaching yoga to children and youth before beginning work. Ideally, this will include some general background in youth development. If this is not the case, yoga service organizations may build this into their in-house training, if they have one. Teachers working solo or with organizations that do not yet have this capacity should seek to educate themselves independently. They should also understand the particularities of the youth justice system and its interface with the "school-to-prison pipeline" in their jurisdiction.[12]

Other key considerations pertinent to teaching youth classes include:

---

12 The term "school-to-prison pipeline" is commonly used to refer to the confluence of laws and policies, and social structures, institutions, and practices that systematically push children and youth (particularly low-income students of color) out of school and into the youth and criminal justice systems. The ACLU offers an excellent set of resources on this topic at https://www.aclu.org/issues/racial-justice/race-and-inequality-education/school-prison-pipeline.

Require Staff Presence. Having facility staff present during yoga classes is a best practice for adults and a nonnegotiable requirement for youth. It is critical to have facility staff supervision at all times when teaching minors in order to protect students and teachers alike, both with regard to liability and in general. Teachers must discontinue class if facility supervision is inadequate (e.g., staff has eyes closed, is deeply engaged in conversation, or on the phone).

The presence of staff during class may have a positive or negative impact on students and class dynamics. This will vary widely and to some extent unpredictably depending on personnel, students, or circumstances. Teachers must practice maximal awareness and full presence to intuit what sort of instructional and interpersonal adjustments are best suited to keep the classroom dynamic in the most optimal zone possible.

Encourage Staff Participation. If feasible and not disruptive of positive class dynamics, having staff participate with youth in yoga classes is recommended. Participating in yoga provides staff with an opportunity to explore the benefits of yoga for themselves, which can support them personally and professionally. Working in facilities is stressful, and yoga offers a vital means of learning to manage stress proactively while supporting overall health and well-being. Such personal benefits can have a positive impact in the workplace by enhancing the capacity of staff members to negotiate challenging situations while reducing health issues and burnout.

Having staff practice yoga together with youth can also improve interpersonal dynamics. Group yoga practices offer a way to share what is often a healing, meaningful experience with others while still maintaining the privacy of each individual's practice. This can create a sense of shared humanity and goodwill that has positive impacts for staff and youth alike.

Be Developmentally Appropriate. Teachers should understand that a student's chronological age may not match his or her developmental one. Early childhood trauma can profoundly effect how youth form relationships, respond to stress, and even govern bodily functions. Disturbances in neuron development can have profound long-term effects on areas of the brain that mediate mood, anxiety, and healthy bonding (Perry, 2006). A 16-year-old may have the speech and language capacity of an 11-year-old and the ability to regulate his or her emotions at the level of a 6-year-old.

Teachers working with youth should teach classes with the needs of their most dysregulated, developmentally youngest students foremost in mind. This includes considering the duration and complexity of a class. For example, an hour-long session may be too much for many, if not most, youth. Beginning with shorter (e.g., 30-minute) classes and, if possible, building from there may be preferable. Similarly, starting out with simple language, concepts, and postures—and growing them slowly and organically over time—will generally be most effective.

Understand Trafficking. Individuals and organizations working with youth should be familiar with commercial sexual exploitation of children (CSEC) and sensitive to its many negative impacts. Research indicates that more than 200,000 children and youth are sex-trafficked in the United States annually. Although CSEC research has typically focused on girls and young women, recent work has expanded to recognize the victimization of boys and young men. While research on male victims of CSEC is limited, new studies suggest that the number of boys and girls involved in child sex trafficking is likely to be similar in numbers (Development Services Group, 2014).

Children and youth who have been victimized by sex trafficking suffer from high rates of PTSD, Stockholm syndrome, memory loss, aggression, fear, depression, anxiety, hostility, anger issues, sexually transmitted disease/infection (STD/STI), physical trauma from beatings, and emotional and psychological trauma from engaging in unwanted sex. Tragically, however, most U.S. jurisdictions treat victims of sex trafficking as offenders. Girls in particular are often picked up for prostitution, charged for selling sex or other related offenses, and kept in custody with little or no access to a support system or treatment options (Development Services Group, 2014).

CURRICULUM AND INSTRUCTION:
BE PUNCTUAL AND PREDICTABLE

Yoga classes should follow an intentional model that maximizes a sense of consistency and predictability for students and staff.

Although predictability is a critical component of any effective trauma-informed yoga class, a correctional facility is an inherently unpredictable teaching environment. Teachers need to be prepared to adjust accordingly, finding ways to maximize a sense of consistency regardless of whatever disruptions and disturbances may occur.

Class plans should be designed with the understanding that starting times may be delayed and classes may be interrupted. Teachers should have the capacity to make adjustments as needed to offer an appropriately sequenced class (e.g., warm up, core practice, cool down, and final relaxation pose) within the time frame available. Instruction should not include long pose sequences that work one side of the body, then the other, as classes may be interrupted or students called out for court or appointments at any time.

Teachers should strive to reframe such unpredictability in ways that support the practice of yoga. Unforeseen challenges are an opportunity to practice equanimity and may offer an important teachable moment. Teachers should be mindful that their work as yoga instructors is to respond, rather than simply react to, whatever arises. Modeling this for students is as much a part of teaching yoga as guiding them through physical postures, if not more.

Be Punctual. Teachers should respect that most facility programs operate on strict schedules, and aim to start and end class on time, regardless of any unexpected disruptions or delays. They should arrive at the facility with sufficient time to get through security and perform whatever room organization is necessary before students are scheduled to arrive. Teachers are wise to factor in extra time to settle into the environment and prepare to teach. In addition to concrete issues such as securing mats, this means consciously taking the time to orient, ground, and center oneself psychologically. Classes should always end punctually unless an explicit agreement has been previously made with the facility and students to extend the time, in which case it should conclude at that time precisely.

Countdown Cues. TIY instruction prioritizes maximizing students' sense of safety, predictability, and control. As much as possible, students should be able to anticipate what is coming next in class. One simple way to support this goal is to avoid holding postures for undefined lengths of time. Instead, teachers can use countdown cues such as "Let's explore how it feels to hold this pose for 5...4... 3...2...1."

CURRICULUM AND INSTRUCTION: EXPECT STUDENT DYNAMICS TO FLUCTUATE

Yoga teachers should understand that student comportment may fluctuate significantly and not take it personally.

It is helpful for yoga teachers to understand that their students are likely to be impacted by the set of social structures and interpersonal dynamics they're enmeshed in on a regular, if unpredictable, basis. This, in turn, should be expected to affect their personal comportment in class. Teachers may find that a student who was fully participatory, cheerful, and even helpful one day is uncommunicative and even rude the next. If this happens, they must learn to not take it personally.

A yoga class may be a space where individuals or groups mix that are otherwise unable to do so. The fact that they are together for yoga doesn't mean that they can interact outside of that room safely. Teachers are wise to be observant to nonverbal cues that may reveal such dynamics. They should never presume to understand the full set of issues that might be at play in any given situation, however.

Students may be detoxing from drugs (street or prescription). They may be taking medications with strong side effects and/or adjusting to new prescriptions. They may have recently been to court. They may have been given upsetting news about friends or family. Another student or staff member may have triggered them. Something deeply upsetting could have happened within their section of the facility.

Usually, there is no way for teachers to know what happened or how to explain changes in students' self-presentation. Nor is it their job to find out. Rather, their charge is to maintain a calm, grounded, and supportive presence regardless of how students present. Again, teachers can and should work with such challenges as opportunities to teach the values of yoga and the skills it instills through the power of example.

Helpful Tools. Although yoga teachers cannot prevent student dynamics from fluctuating, they can lay a foundation that supports a better connection to them irrespective of changing conditions. Concrete steps to consider include:

- **Understand facility rules** governing whether students are allowed to take class. Be aware of any relevant institutional reward systems in place. Work to build relationships with facility staff who support equal access to yoga for all students.

- **Develop a student intake form** that asks for information about preferred name, preferred gender pronouns, medical issues, and "anything else you want me to know." (Note: Forms should be simple, designed with potential literacy barriers in mind. Facility staff will likely want to review and approve any such forms prior to use.)

- **Attend multidisciplinary team (MDT) meetings** if they exist at your site and allow your participation. Traditionally, MDTs are groups of health care workers situated in different disciplines (psychiatry, social work, etc.) who try to coordinate services while treating patients in their area of expertise. In facilities, MDTs may include probation officers, mental health professionals, and community-based organizations.

Although MDTs do not exist at every facility, yoga teachers are encouraged to work to be invited and recognized as a valuable member of the "team" where possible. (If only professional staff attend, volunteer teachers may be considered ineligible.) MDT meetings can provide important insights into students' backgrounds and behaviors, as well as an opportunity to explore the benefits of collaborative troubleshooting.

- **Avoid the small battles** and focus relentlessly on the bigger picture of sharing the benefits of yoga. For example, students may not be comfortable removing socks or shoes because of culture, safety, and hygiene concerns. If this is the case, teachers should be accepting. Such relatively small deviations from standard procedure may be accommodated in whatever way works, provided facility rules are respected.

Group Dynamics. It's important that teachers understand that the class as a whole will have an evolving dynamic, which is normal. Periods of pushback or withdrawal from participants should be expected and not taken personally.

Understanding that class dynamics tend to shift over time is particularly vital for teachers working with stable or semi-stable groups, as there is a tendency to assume that the same set of students should settle into some predictable behavioral pattern quickly. Research on group dynamics demonstrates, however, that such presumptions of stability are likely to be proven wrong.

Social scientists have identified four primary stages of group development: forming, storming, norming, and performing. "Forming" focuses on acceptance and approval, and decisions of whether to commit to the group. In the second stage, "storming," the group shifts from a focus on group acceptance, approval, commitment, and norms to a preoccupation with dominance, control, and power. This phase is characterized by conflict among group members or between them and their leader (Yalom, 1985, p. 297). Clearly, this "storming" stage could be challenging for a yoga teacher to navigate!

Teachers can take heart, however, in the knowledge that subsequent stages are easier. "Norming" refers to the establishment of group cohesion, and "performing" refers to the development of group competencies and insights (Yalom, 1985, p. 297). Ideally, yoga classes will settle into these latter, smoother stages without undue struggle. Again, however, teachers should expect even well-normed classes to experience fluctuations in both individual and group dynamics.

CURRICULUM AND INSTRUCTION: NAVIGATE POWER DIFFERENTIALS SKILLFULLY

Yoga teachers should be sensitive to the inherent power differential between them and their students, and work to navigate it skillfully.

Like any form of instruction, yoga classes tend to create a power differential between teachers and students. This is true no matter where classes are taught. This standard power imbalance is exacerbated in the context of correctional facilities, however, for multiple reasons. Most obvious, the teacher is free to come and go voluntarily, whereas students are involuntarily detained. Real or perceived power differences around issues of race, gender (identity or expression), age, socioeconomic status, and other factors may also be in play. Teachers should strive to be sensitive to these dynamics and work to navigate any real or perceived power differential skillfully.

It's important for teachers to accept their status and work with it in ways that model healthy power dynamics of responsibility and accountability, as opposed to unhealthy ones of domination and arbitrary control. To pretend that the inherent power differential between teachers and students doesn't exist or can be eliminated may cause problems. Those unwilling or unable to assume the authority inherent in the teacher may (with the best of intentions) wind up shirking their responsibilities.

Teachers should be aware that students, staff, and others may consciously or unconsciously project expectations on them. What this involves will vary from person to person. One image that is commonly projected onto yoga teachers is that of the "all-knowing healer." Such projection is natural and can be an important part of the awakening of a person's own innate "all-knowing healer" within. Alternatively, it could feed into patterns of a codependent or exploitive relationship. Teachers must be consistently engaged in their own processes of self-reflection, learning, and growth in order to keep relationships with students and others healthy and empowering for all concerned.

Conscious Relationship. Yoga service is predicated on a commitment to service as a form of "conscious relationship," which recognizes and respects differences while rejecting any form of hierarchy that holistically positions one person above or below another (Childress & Cohen Harper, 2016). Conscious relationship requires yoga teachers to practice self-awareness and self-reflection on many levels. Doing so in ways that help establish a horizontal relationship of service, rather than a vertical one of "helping" or "charity," is an indispensible component of the teaching process (Remen, n.d.).

This is not to suggest that teachers should not assume appropriate authority or refuse to "own their power" as teachers. Instead, it is to emphasize that this can be achieved without creating a rigid sense of hierarchy, in which teachers seem to be placed on a plane far above and apart from their students. In trauma-informed practice, the hierarchy of teacher-student relationships is functional. Teachers are there to be helpful guides not dictatorial authorities.

Simple ways in which teachers can practice conscious relationship include greeting students as they come in the room and thanking them for having come to class before they leave. The basic human connection of a warm greeting or farewell can go a long way. Often, it helps people feel that they are seen and that their presence is valued.

As much as possible, teachers should treat each person who comes to class equally. Praising one student may unintentionally reinforce the negative self-talk of another.

Apologize Appropriately. If language or other mistakes are made, teachers may seek to model the strength of a genuine apology. One example might be, "I'm sorry for assuming that, thanks for explaining further what you meant."

Teachers should be aware of any tendencies to over-apologize. This is a very common occurrence, especially when teachers are working outside of their race, culture, and/or socioeconomic background. In instances that involve a white person teaching students of color, it can be an example of what has been termed "white fragility." Teachers should be aware that students may find over-apologizing off-putting or even insulting. Some may see it as a weakness to be leveraged and exploited. It is important to remain appropriately specific in whatever apology is offered.

Practice Humility. Language often has impacts that we do not foresee or intend. While teachers should work to familiarize themselves with the culture and communication styles of those they are teaching and otherwise encountering, they should remember that they don't know people's stories, experiences, and histories. It's important to not make assumptions.

Teachers are encouraged to take ownership of their words and actions, and always have a beginner's mind. They should practice remaining inquisitive, supporting reciprocal relationships and open conversation, and remaining open to learning from their students and others.

Have Fun. In a justice setting, the environment and circumstances can be grim. Offering yoga in ways that include light-heartedness, good-natured humor, and a sense of noncompetitive play is healing and beneficial. The value of practicing yoga in ways that generate energies of vitality, fun, and even joy is inestimable.

CURRICULUM AND INSTRUCTION: SUPPORT SELF-REGULATION

Teachers should understand the neurobiology of trauma and how to sequence classes that support students' capacities for self-regulation.

As discussed in the preceding chapter, a high proportion of incarcerated people have experienced complex trauma. Yoga teachers consequently need to understand the neurobiology of trauma and how to sequence classes in ways that support students' capacities for self-regulation.

Complex trauma impacts the brain and development of the nervous system in ways that undermine the ability to regulate emotions and take in information. The instinctual core of the brain becomes wired to remain constantly on alert for harm or threat, with the fight-flight-freeze stress response stuck in overdrive. This makes it difficult, if not impossible, to process incoming stimuli appropriately and have adaptive responses to day-to-day stress. Instead, there is a tendency to either overreact to stressors with aggression or hostility, or underreact by "numbing out" with dissociative behavior. At the same time, the ability to access the brain's higher cognitive centers, where new learning and personal reflection occurs, can be impeded.

Neurobiology of Trauma. Yoga classes should be sequenced with this neurobiology of trauma in mind. The foundational principle must be to maximize the safety of the classroom environment. The more that people feel safe, the more the brain's fight-flight-freeze response is subdued. This allows greater access to more nuanced feelings and higher-order cognitive capacities for thinking and learning.

A good rubric for remembering how to sequence appropriately is the "Three Rs":

1. First, *Regulate;*

2. Then, *Relate;*

3. And finally, *Reason.*

This order follows the "bottom-up" theory of how the human brain developed over time, which forms the deeper scientific basis for this understanding of trauma.

First, the brain developed its most basic, survival-oriented capacities (fight, flight, or freeze). This part of the brain must be *regulated* (the first "R") before it's possible to work with the next part of the brain to develop, which governs its more sensate, emotional capacities. This is the second "R" of *relating* to oneself and others. Once the parts of the brain that correspond to the first two "Rs" are on line, it's possible to work more fruitfully with its higher-order thinking skills and rational, analytic capacities. This, of course, corresponds to the third "R" of *reason.*

Appropriately sequenced yoga classes support this process of bottom-up brain regulation. The first "R" should be supported by "self-regulation techniques," including simple breathing and movement exercises pulled from a standard yoga *asana* and *pranayama* repertoire. Here, the focus is on reducing an overactive sympathetic nervous system and supporting the activation of the parasympathetic nervous system (e.g., breathing techniques that encourage a longer exhalation than inhalation). Self-regulation can also be supported by "sensory-integration techniques" such as soothing music, self-massage, and essential oils (if approved by the facility and chosen by the student), which work through the five senses to calm the nervous system.

Once regulation is supported, yoga teachers can work with the second "R" of *relating.* Typically, this includes introducing more poses and cues designed to help students develop interoceptive, or internal awareness, skills. Over time, students can develop the capacity to connect to internal sensations and feelings while remaining grounded and self-regulated. This ability is not only intrinsic to healing trauma but to becoming more self-aware and able to reflect and respond to events in more deliberate, considered ways.

In addition to learning to relate better to one's self, the second "R" refers to the ability to relate more with others. In the context of a yoga class, this means that any interpersonal communication exercises, such as verbal "check-ins" and "check-outs," may be best implemented after the students have been led through more foundational self-regulating and sensory-integrating experiences. (Note: This depends in part on the intended purpose of the verbal communication.

For example, simple verbal "check-ins" at the very beginning of class may help establish a sense of connection and build trust with groups of students who are new to yoga.)

Generally speaking, the third "R" of *reason* will be less emphasized in a yoga class. Teachers should be aware, however, that class components that require some higher-order thinking capacities—such as learning the benefits of a posture or more-sophisticated *pranayama* techniques—should be avoided early in class or when students appear dysregulated, as they require calmer emotional states and higher cognitive functioning.

CURRICULUM AND INSTRUCTION: UNDERSTAND "TRIGGERS"

Teachers should understand what triggers are, how to minimize them, and how to respond if they occur.

Trauma symptoms can be "triggered" at any moment by a variety of unpredictable factors. While striving to minimize triggers in their classroom space and teaching methods, teachers must accept that there is no way to ensure a trigger-free environment. Common triggers experienced in correctional facilities include:

- Small spaces

- Loud noises

- Restrained physical movement

- Lack of privacy

- Strip searches

- Misperceptions of others' behaviors

- Aggressive or abusive peers or facility staff

- Subtle nuances such as a tone of voice or mannerism reminiscent of an abuser

Teachers need to understand how to identify signs that a student has been triggered. Typically, this will manifest in one of two types of intensified nervous system dysregulation: 1) *hyperarousal,* which is often expressed through anger, hostility, defiance, and so on; or 2) *hypoarousal,* which can show up as increased fidgeting, upward gaze, distractibility, disconnection, and the like.

In the absence of a trauma-informed lens, people's reaction to triggers or attempts to manage them (whether in yoga classes or elsewhere) are often perceived as defiant, aggressive, or rude. Proficiency in TIY enables teachers to depersonalize such behaviors and respond to them appropriately. Rather than reacting negatively, such teachers understand that students with unprocessed trauma are managing a lot of physiological dysregulation and feelings of overwhelm. TIY-trained instructors are able to offer students simple breathing, movement, and attention tools that support self-regulation and a sense of safety. This can be a profoundly useful and even healing experience for them.

Triggering Poses. A high percentage of incarcerated and court-involved people are survivors of sexual trauma. As such, they are likely to have developed coping adaptations that dissociate them from their bodies. Yoga teachers must understand that guiding students to connect to their bodies' "felt sense" (also called "embodying" or "interoception") is only healing under conditions that maximize psychological and emotional safety. If pushed too quickly or insensitively, such reconnection to bodily feelings and sensations can be threatening, and they may trigger traumatic memories.

Teachers may find it helpful to guide students to notice what might be feeling good, strong, or neutral in their bodies during the beginning portion of the class. The more students are able to establish a visceral sense of connection to what feels good inside their bodies, the more they may be able to tolerate uncomfortable sensations that may arise during the course of the yoga practice without being overwhelmed by them. This ability to experience discomfort without feeling swept away by it is crucial to the process of healing trauma, and it's a skill with enormous potential benefits for everyday life "off the mat."

Certain yoga poses should only be taught very cautiously, if at all. Generally speaking, postures that expose emotionally sensitive areas of the body should either be avoided or adapted to support psychological safety. For example, clasping hands behind one's back (such as in *Shalabasana*) simulates an arrest and should generally be avoided for incarcerated students. Downward-Facing Dog can be avoided if doing it would put students in a position where their backsides are facing a door or staff. Providing options to opt out of different positions and/or movements is always important.

> "Even a yoga posture as benign as Savasana [lying on the back with arms and legs extended] can retrigger a survivor of sexual trauma. But offering simple options such as crossing the ankles, bringing the hands over the heart, or opting to lay on the belly or do seated meditation instead can completely shift the experience in a positive direction."

Breath Work. Breathing exercises also require special consideration. For example, research shows that the incarcerated population disproportionately suffers from anxiety and asthma. Consequently, teachers must be careful when it comes to *pranayama* techniques that focus on the upper chest or utilize breath retention, which could be triggering. Breathing cues should also be employed mindfully to avoid language that may feel overly directive or controlling.

If attempting to breathe deeply seems to increase students' anxiety or arousal, it can be useful to have them focus on "grounding," or directing their attention to feel how their bodies are in contact with and supported by the floor. Often, breathing opens up after grounding is established.

As a general rule, breathing should be taught in ways that support a free and expansive feeling for students, not a tight and restrictive one.

Avoid Long Silences. Teachers are advised to avoid long silences in their classes, as they could trigger a dissociative response. This may mean that parts of yoga classes that would normally have sustained silence, like seated meditation and final relaxation pose, should be handled differently than in a studio or gym class.

One option might be to play music with intentional, inspirational lyrics, provided that the facility allows it and students feel it is a good choice. Be aware that popular music has more potential to be triggering, as it's more likely to carry strong associations to feelings and memories.

Another option is to offer guided meditations such as body scans or *yoga nidra*. Here, it's recommended to provide verbal cues and offer visualizations that maintain students' sense of connection with their own physicality and the present moment, which mitigates the trauma response. Directing student attention to more typically sensitive areas of the body such as the throat or pelvic region, should, however, be avoided, at least with newer students.

Nature-based "journeys" or other exercises exploring an imaginary, out-of-body landscape are best avoided, as they may encourage a sense of disconnection and disassociation, and/or remind students of negative experiences that occurred in such environments in the past.

CURRICULUM AND INSTRUCTION: OFFER CHOICE

Yoga teachers should consistently encourage students to make simple but meaningful choices concerning their practice throughout class.

Incarcerated people have very few opportunities to exercise personal choice in their day-to-day lives. Correctional facilities enforce regulations and restrictions governing what they can and cannot do. Their time is tightly structured and controlled. They experience little to no privacy. They can be searched or put in solitary confinement without warning. Their contact with the outside world is strictly limited.

Yoga classes can be a time when students are offered some much-needed opportunities for personal decision-making. To facilitate this experience, teachers
should consistently use invitational rather than commanding language. For example, it is preferable to say, "If you feel comfortable closing your eyes, I invite
you to do so. If not, you can perhaps let your gaze soften and move downward,"
as opposed to simply saying, "Close your eyes" (a common directive in most
yoga classes).

Although seemingly a small gesture, being consistently encouraged to feel into
what is most appropriate for one's body and mind on a moment-to-moment
basis can be a powerful tool in healing trauma, reducing reactivity, and enhancing self-awareness. As such, it supports the development of self-regulation
skills that are profoundly helpful in everyday life, enabling students to access
greater degrees of awareness, reflection, and choice—even under stress and in
challenging conditions.

Pose Options. It's a best practice to provide simple pose options gauged to correspond with students' differing levels of physical ability. In doing so, instructors
should take care to avoid language that suggests a spectrum from "beginning"
to "advanced" options, focusing instead on encouraging students to feel into
their experience and respond to it by selecting the appropriate alternative for
that moment.

Any student who prefers to be in a resting pose, rather than in an active one,
should be encouraged to do so. It is helpful to mention this at the beginning of
the class and repeat it throughout. Simply being present in the calm of a yoga
class can have a healing effect. It is not necessary for students to perform every
(or even any) physical postures, provided they are respectful of others and not
disrupting the class.

Religious Concerns. Students will have a variety of personal beliefs when it
comes to questions of religion, spirituality, and secularism. Some may be concerned that yoga is some sort of religiously inflected practice that violates their
faith commitments. Teachers may consider addressing this issue proactively by

explaining that yoga is not a religion but instead a practice of coming into deeper connection with our "best selves." This message could either be communicated verbally or in a "welcome letter" to students.

It is important to reflect on what types of instruction might unintentionally cause students to feel that their faith boundaries are being compromised, and then proactively address it. For example, asking students to chant in Sanskrit, while common in some yoga methods, could legitimately be seen as a religious practice. Teachers should refrain from such instruction unless they know for certain that all students understand and feel comfortable with it.

Some poses may also raise religious concerns. For example, students may not want to do Child's Pose (a resting posture that involves sitting back on the feet, stretching the torso and arms forward, and resting the head on the ground) because it is similar to a religiously significant prostration. Or they may be opposed to bringing hands together at the heart in a prayer-like position.

Offering choice often works to mitigate concerns. For example, students might be comfortable with chanting "Om" if it is explicitly stated that those who prefer to chant another (complementary and nondisruptive) sound or stay silent are welcome to do so.

CURRICULUM AND INSTRUCTION:
USE LANGUAGE INTENTIONALLY

Yoga teachers should always use language that is simple, invitational, and respectful.

The starting point for effective yoga instruction is authenticity. As discussed repeatedly throughout this book, teachers should practice self-inquiry and learning about the system they're working in on a regular, ongoing basis. This combination of individual reflection and social education will help teachers find and sustain their authentic voice.

Invitational language is a foundation of trauma-informed yoga instruction. Many yoga classes taught in studios, gyms, and so on, utilize command-style language (e.g., "Close your eyes," as opposed to "If you're comfortable closing your eyes, you are invited to do so. If not, you are free to let your gaze soften and move downward.") Because trauma involves a loss of autonomous choice and control, providing students with ongoing opportunities to exercise simple choices and control their own practice is therapeutic. Invitational language featuring simple choice options is particularly critical given that trauma makes it extremely difficult, if not impossible, for people to feel "at home" in their bodies. TIY is an important resource for shifting this relationship with the embodied self in a healthy, positive direction.

Teachers should also consider the following recommendations for verbal instruction:

- **Strive for Clarity.** Teachers should endeavor to use language that is simple, concise, and direct. Repetition is good. Potentially ambiguous terms may either be defined in advance or avoided. Esoteric "yoga speak" (e.g., "Mother Earth") feed into yoga stereotypes and should be avoided.

- **Explain Benefits.** Studies show that people are more likely to continue doing something (such as adopting yoga as a lifestyle tool) if they understand why they are doing it. Consequently, it's recommended that teachers explain why certain poses or yoga in general is beneficial in reasonably detailed, descriptive ways. At the same time, teachers must be careful to avoid any language that communicates to students that they "should" feel a certain way or receive particular benefits.

- **Normalize Discomfort.** Some students may find that the yoga practice initially connects them to how bad they feel. It's important for teachers to normalize that experience as not necessarily uncommon or bad. To the extent students are able to retain a sense of basic safety and grounding, encouraging them to stay present with discomforting feelings and move through them rather than avoid them, is important, as the ability to do so is central to the healing dimensions of yoga. To support this ability, teachers should regularly emphasize self-compassion as a core aspect of the practice.

- **Encourage Inquiry.** Encourage students to "own" their yoga experience as an opportunity to come into the present moment and learn about themselves, both physically and beyond. Teachers should avoid communicating that postures "should" generate certain feelings or benefits (e.g., saying, "You will notice this in your hips"). Instead, they can ask students to self-assess with cues such as: "How does this feel?" "What are you noticing?" "What's happening in your body?"

- **Be Responsive.** Be creative in adapting language to fit students' culture, circumstances, and experiences. For example, consider using "brave space" instead of "safe space" (since teachers can't truly offer safety in facilities or other criminal justice system settings) or substitute "Wisdom Pose" for "Child's Pose" (as this may more clearly communicate honor and respect).

- **Be Inclusive.** Teachers should strive for inclusive language (e.g., "we" versus "you") and reflect on which terms work best in their particular context (e.g., "folks," "y'all," "everyone," "all," and "let's"). If preferred gender pronouns have been established, they should be used. If not, gender-neutral language is recommended.

As noted earlier, teachers are advised to avoid language that implies hierarchies of achievement within yoga practice, particularly in referring to physical postures (e.g., "beginning" versus "advanced" pose options). Rather than offering choices based on a perceived scale of mastery, instructors should utilize language that encourages sensitive tracking of and response to sensations, capacities, and limitations on a moment-by-moment basis.

- **Be Body Positive.** Struggles with body image are epidemic in society today. Teachers should reflect on whether they have their own body image issues that may be unconsciously communicated to students, and take corrective action if needed. Teachers should also be aware that students of all genders may be struggling with these issues in ways that are difficult to identify and address.

To counter the cultural power of unrealistic and damaging expectations, teachers should always speak respectfully of all body types, appearances, and abilities—both their own and those of others. It is also important to avoid making or communicating unwarranted assumptions that certain types of bodies will be more able or more limited than others.

- **Name Body Parts Mindfully.** When instructing movement or guiding students through internal "body scans" (i.e., directing mental attention toward feeling into different parts of the body), it's important to describe body parts using language that's as general and as non-sexually charged as possible to avoid triggering. For example, refer to the "hip area," rather than the "butt."

- **Understand Slang.** Teachers are encouraged to familiarize themselves with jargon and slang used by their students. If students use terms teachers don't understand, teachers may ask them to explain it. Teachers should avoid using slang themselves, however, unless it feels truly authentic to their personal history and experience.

> "In my youth detention classes, when I ask for one word to describe how my students feel, I often get, 'booling,' which I learned is a combo of cool and chilling (meaning calm or relaxed), 'tight' (upset), and 'ard' or 'aight' (alright)."

CURRICULUM AND INSTRUCTION: CAREFULLY CONSIDER THE USE OF TOUCH

Yoga service organizations and independent teachers should develop policies concerning the use of touch in yoga classes carefully.

The use of hands-on "adjustments," in which yoga teachers place their hands on students to guide them into a pose or offer other sorts of tactile feedback and instruction, is common in mainstream yoga classes. Much of the trauma-sensitive yoga field, however, has recommended avoiding any such use of touch due to its high potential for retriggering trauma (Emerson and Hopper, 2011).

Some expert teachers and yoga service providers who specialize in criminal justice work feel strongly that touch should be prohibited in yoga instruction under all circumstances. Others believe that touch can be beneficial, particularly for the sensory-integrating, relational aspects of healing for neurodevelopmental trauma (Perry, 2006), provided that appropriate training and protocols are in place. The use of touch in yoga instruction is a highly contentious issue in the field and will almost certainly remain so for the foreseeable future.

Review Principles. Yoga service providers who wish to consider the use of touch in the course of yoga instruction should review the following principles and questions carefully before making any decisions:

- **Understand institutional policy pertaining to touch between yoga teachers and students, and among students themselves.** Teachers must know all the relevant rules and regulations regarding human contact in the facility where they serve. Many facilities do not allow any physical touch between providers and students, beyond a handshake. As discussed repeatedly throughout this book, such strictures must be followed precisely, consistently, and without exception.

- **Be aware that incarcerated persons may not have the capacity to provide informed consent.** In many jurisdictions, incarcerated individuals legally do not have the capacity to consent. For example, they may not have the capacity to refuse care or treatment, and may have a limited capacity to consent to participation in research.

Understand Consent. While yoga instruction is not legally regulated, there are parallel issues that need to be considered. Consent involves the capacity to choose freely, without coercion and undue influence. Incarcerated individuals live in conditions that severely restrict their autonomy and may impose undue pressures (real or perceived) when it comes to consent. Even if instructors seek permission of students for the use of touch, it's possible that they may feel pressured to accept it for reasons the teacher doesn't understand. Consequently, it's imperative to be extra-cautious around the use of touch in these settings.

Assess Carefully. If touch is allowed in the facility, yoga providers should carefully consider the following questions:

- Do the benefits of touch outweigh the potential harm and retriggering of trauma for this population?

- What is the gender expression of the teachers and students? Does this configuration make the situation safer or more likely to trigger trauma?

- What is the individual and/or organizational liability regarding touch?

- What is the level of facility staff supervision? Will staff be supervising classes sufficiently such that if a student accuses a teacher of improper touch, staff could serve as a legitimate eyewitness?

"Learning to teach with verbal cues as opposed to touch can be incredibly empowering to the student. It might be construed that the student is 'doing it wrong' and that the teacher is 'fixing' them if there are hands-on adjustments. Offering a verbal cue and then having the student execute it is an incredible teachable moment for all."

If there is a decision to include touch in yoga instruction, yoga providers should strongly consider the following:

- Teachers need to be trained on how and when to do trauma-informed adjustments. An essential part of their training should include sexual trauma.

- Students should never be touched unless the teacher asks and is given permission first.

- If possible, adjustment cards (small chips or cards that students use to give teachers a clear "yes" or "no" concerning touch) should be used. (Note: This may require staff approval in many facilities, if it's feasible at all.)

- Teachers should avoid adjusting all students in initial classes and any newcomers in established ones. Touch may only commence after students have been participating in classes for some time and a good rapport with the teacher established.

- Adjustments should be kept simple and made with clear, slightly firm, and purposeful movement.

- Language around touch should be kept appropriate and consistent. For example, if students refer to it as "massage," the teacher can gently correct them with the term "adjustment."

- Often, the best adjustments are those that empower students by giving them control. For example, the teacher can hold a hand out and offer a student the option of "trying to push into my hand." Or students could be asked to move toward an open palm (by bending their knee, lifting their head, reaching their fingers, etc.), which can be gently moved away before physical touch occurs. Such methods enable students to "own" the experience, instead of having something "done" to them.

- The timing of hands-on adjustments should be considered carefully. Utilizing them later in class, if and when students are more regulated, tends to work best.

- Teachers should not approach students from the back to offer an adjustment. Students should be easily able to see their instructors coming.

- If an adjustment elicits an untoward reaction from students, teachers should apologize and allow space for them to recover, initiating trauma-response protocols if necessary.

- Consider alternatives to touch such as use of verbal cues, self-massage, or partner work (with discretion and only if the facility allows it).

Special Considerations for Youth. Human contact is a primary and essential need, and is particularly important for youth who have experienced trauma and deprivation. At the same time, issues of consent are particularly thorny for those under age 18, as their legal rights may be more constrained, and personal maturity and self-confidence less developed.

A primary argument in favor of using touch in youth classes is that younger persons are at much higher risk of experiencing unsafe touch (such as violence or sexual exploitation) in the future. Giving them the opportunity to learn to recognize positive and safe touch can be preventive, and provide a healing, reparative experience from past trauma (Jackson, 2009).

A primary argument against the use of touch in yoga classes with youth is that they are even more constrained in their sense of agency vis-à-vis an adult teacher than incarcerated adults. Again, this is a contentious issue in the field that provokes sharp disagreement even among highly experienced teachers and other experts.

CURRICULUM AND INSTRUCTION: SUPPORT STUDENT EMPOWERMENT

Yoga teachers should look for opportunities to empower and lift up students.

The criminal justice environment can be oppressive and disempowering. To the extent that it is safe, appropriate, undisruptive of student relationships, and in conformance with facility rules and regulations, yoga teachers are wise to seek out opportunities to support student empowerment by providing support, encouragement, and resources for them to practice yoga on their own and with others. Teachers should also strive to connect yoga with other parts of student lives that support personal growth.

> "One of the school teachers at our youth facility told us that a girl in her class led the whole group in a deep breathing exercise before they took a test together."

Teachers can also seek ways to empower students as nascent teachers in the context of class. For example, interested students could be guided to teach particular segments such as a posture or sequence. Teachers could also ask students to suggest music or read their own poetry in class. (Both should be vetted by the teacher first to avoid anything potentially triggering for fellow students or prohibited by the facility.) As discussed in chapter 7, well-established yoga service organizations might also consider developing a yoga teacher training for dedicated students within interested facilities.

Teachers should approach the empowering of their students with a sensitivity to facility rules that prohibit incarcerated individuals from taking any type of leadership position. The social dynamics in play in the teacher-student relationship when a yoga instructor comes in "from the outside" versus when one incarcerated individual teaches others are entirely different and should not be underestimated. It is vital to be sensitive to power dynamics within facilities and to consider any actions that might disrupt existing patterns very carefully. (For more on this subject, see chapter 7, "Facility-Based Yoga Teacher Trainings.)

4

RELATIONSHIP BUILDING

While the criminal justice system is indeed a system, it is nonetheless one composed of individual human beings. Looking at the system from afar, the human experience of the people involved—on all sides—can get lost. Recognizing and respecting the humanity of each individual involved in this often dehumanizing system is the overarching best practice for building relationships that support quality yoga offerings within it.

It's vital to understand the staggering statistics on American incarceration rates, as well as the economic and political issues bound up with them. But it's equally crucial to go beyond the numbers to see the individual human beings involved. Otherwise, it's all-too-easy to view incarcerated people, as well as facility administration and staff, through a lens of preexisting bias and stereotyping. Such shortsightedness creates profound obstacles to empathetically relating to the many unique human beings who are part of this system.

Many established practices and attitudes reinforce such biases and contribute to a culture of dehumanization. Incarcerated people are assigned a number for tracking. They are stripped of their civilian clothes and issued a standard uniform. They are commonly referred to by staff using only their last name, a practice that is often not merely custom but policy. Those held in solitary confinement are isolated from most contact with other people for days, weeks, and years.

Dehumanization is not limited to the incarcerated. The people who work in the system also tend to be viewed through a myopic lens. They may wear a uniform and, like the people they supervise, are typically referred to only by rank and last name. Correctional officers may be seen in deeply negative terms regardless of who they are or how their work is conducted. There may be little or no interest in understanding the particularities of their lives, histories, and communities.

Yoga teachers working in the criminal justice system may also be seen through a biased lens, derided as "hug-a-thug" do-gooders or dismissed as flighty lightweights.

Yoga itself may be preemptively judged as a practice that is undeserving of study based on stereotypes rather than any real knowledge of the practice. Due to the ubiquity of highly commercialized yoga imagery, many people both inside and outside the criminal justice system have come to see yoga as the exclusive domain of affluent young white women, who are themselves perceived more as stereotypes than real human beings. Cutting through such preconceptions may take time and determination.

All the people involved with the criminal justice system—whether as yoga teachers, correctional staff, court personnel, incarcerated persons, or others—are nonetheless unique human beings with their own histories, personal orientations, strengths, weaknesses, and perspectives. The more that this basic yet essential truth is not only remembered but actively realized in practice, the better the relationship-building process will be. Positive interpersonal relationships are crucial to quality yoga instruction, individual healing, and healthy organizational development. Consequently, a commitment to humanization is the necessary foundation of any good work to be done.

RELATIONSHIP BUILDING: PRACTICE SELF-REFLECTION AND SELF-INQUIRY

Yoga teachers should have a "deep practice" that includes ongoing self-reflection and self-inquiry.

The Yoga Service Council's working definition of yoga service recognizes self-inquiry as a foundation supporting the conscious relationship in which the practice is best offered:

> We naturally offer the practices (and create our programs) through our own lens—from the perspective of our history, privilege, bias, and wisdom. We offer yoga mixed with all the other things we know and have experienced in our lives. A commitment to reflection and self-inquiry allows yoga service providers to engage skillfully, honestly, and authentically with students, regardless of whether teacher and students come from similar life circumstances. It helps us look closely at what we know and don't know about ourselves, those we serve and teach, and the communities we engage with. It is training to better understand our own perspective and the perspectives of our students (Childress & Cohen Harper, 2016, p. 2).

A yoga teacher's capacity to hold space for others is directly related to his or her capacity to hold space for him- or herself. Yoga service providers are encouraged to practice recognizing their own biases and judgments, understanding and communicating their personal needs, and bringing the shadow aspects of their personalities into the light. They should also have developed a strong understanding of their own experiences of trauma, how they tend to be triggered, and how to work with self-regulating practices as needed. Such work frees them to serve others more openly, consciously, and effectively.

The more teachers harbor unmet needs and leave shadow aspects of their personalities uninvestigated, the more these unconscious parts of their beings will cause problems. One way or another, these unintegrated dimensions of one's inner life will find expression. For yoga teachers, this means that any service work is likely to be offered with "strings attached." A committed, ongoing practice of self-reflection and self-inquiry is necessary to minimize such problems.

"Deep Practice." Such self-reflection and self-inquiry can be supported through a "deep practice" of mindful yoga. As traditionally understood, the practice of yoga is a process of deepening the relationship with the self. As we come to see the many dimensions of ourselves more clearly—including our own individual and cultural histories—our capacity to relate to others in more clear-sighted ways expands as well. Acknowledging our own orientations and biases allows us to enter into relationships with others with greater authenticity (Sherts, 2009).

Mindfulness supports an ability to recognize habitual reactions, including those brought out through service work in a challenging environment. Often, when yoga teachers find themselves reacting to a relationship in this context, it is because they have come up against an edge of fear of "the other" that is in inherent in their preexisting bias.

Teachers who find themselves activated (experiencing innate fear responses, self-critical voices, strong attachments to the outcome, reactions to others' traumatic experiences, excessively strong judgments, etc.) should remember that they can rely on the same yoga practices they teach to self-regulate. For teachers and students alike, developing the ability to self-regulate in challenging situations frees them to choose considered responses rather than simply react blindly to events.

Motivation and Outcome. There are many ways to serve in the yoga world. Not every teacher is well suited to work in the criminal justice system. The system itself is also varied; not everyone is equipped to work well with every population or in every location within it. This is okay, provided that teachers have the capacity to recognize their own limitations and to be honest with themselves and others about them.

Teachers should realize that many strong feelings are likely to arise in the course of doing this work. They may be triggered, feel love, experience anger, and more. This is all normal.

That said, teachers should strive to be aware of what is driving their motivation to teach yoga in this setting, as this will shape how they show up and the outcomes of their actions. While the intention of each teacher or program may be a bit different, the unifying factor should be that yoga service is offered in the spirit of supporting the empowerment and well-being of the individual and community engaged in the practice. Doing this in a way that goes beyond words to lived reality requires a level of self-knowledge and honesty that is not always easy to access.

The World Health Organization defines mental health as:

> *a state of well-being in which every individual realizes his or her own potential, can cope with the normal stresses of life, can work, productively and fruitfully, and is able to make a contribution to her or his community.*

It's important that yoga service providers be vigilant about identifying motivations that fall outside of this "spirit of supporting empowerment and well-being." Are teachers looking to "fix" or "save" others? Are they seeking an outlet for their anger at the system? Do they feel guilty because of their privilege? Do they believe that doing this work will qualify them as a "good person"?

As long as such problematic motivations are honestly recognized and worked through, they are not necessarily disqualifiers. However, if they fester unacknowledged, they most likely indicate a lack of fit for the work at hand.

Teachers who harbor motivations they are unaware of cannot engage in intentional relationships of empowerment that adequately support and foster the well-being of those they are dedicated to serve. Criminal justice professionals and yoga service organizations should consequently be prepared to dismiss teachers who demonstrate an inability to engage with themselves and others in ways that truly support the empowerment and well-being of their students.

RELATIONSHIP BUILDING: PRACTICE SELF-CARE

Yoga service providers should understand and put into action the principle that supporting others requires engaging in regular practices of self-care.

Self-care is not selfish. The effects of undischarged stress can accumulate quickly and degrade our capacity to engage with others as unique human beings deserving of recognition and respect. For yoga teachers, unprocessed stress undercuts their ability to "hold space" for their students to explore their practice in healing, empowering ways. While self-care is important for everyone, it is particularly crucial for yoga service providers responsible for guiding and supporting others on a regular basis.

While the fundamentals of self-care are not complicated in theory, they are often difficult to realize in practice. The following components of a solid self-care regime are particularly important to consider and work on regularly.

Rest. Yoga teachers should get an adequate amount of quality sleep to restore mind and body. Those who have trouble sleeping are encouraged to research and practice good sleep hygiene. It's also important to recognize that insomnia may be a symptom of secondary trauma.

Exercise. It's no secret that regular exercise promotes physical, mental, and emotional well-being. Yoga is great exercise and has the added benefit of supporting stress reduction. Also consider walking, hiking, biking, kayaking, playing tennis, volleyball, basketball, gardening, dancing, surfing, and the like.

In addition to dedicated time for regular exercise, building healthy movement into a daily routine by taking the stairs instead of the elevator, biking instead of driving, adding stretching breaks into computer time, and so on is very valuable.

Hydration and Nutrition. Staying hydrated and eating a healthy diet are important parts of self-care. Drinking enough water is essential. The best indication of proper hydration is the color of one's urine. If the urine is dark yellow or amber in color, drink more water. If it's clear, then consider cutting back.

What precisely constitutes a healthy diet is beyond the scope of this book. Noted food author Michael Pollan offers this simple advice in his book *In Defense of*

Food: "Eat food, not too much, mostly plants." Avoid refined sugars, fast food, and highly processed foods. Stop eating before feeling completely full.

Although food is obviously a basic survival need, it also has crucial social and emotional dimensions. Consider the emotional benefit of sharing meals with others and taking the time to talk about and share one's day. Understand the emotional value of periodically allowing oneself to indulge in some favorite food, even if it doesn't fall into the realm of a "healthy" diet.

Stress Reduction. Yoga can be enormously effective in relieving stress. Readers who are unfamiliar with the practice themselves may wish to consider exploring some simple, beginning practices to see whether it works for them.

Keep in mind that there are many different yoga styles and methods, including gentle movements that can be done while seated in a chair, highly athletic sequences that provide a strong workout, and more. Remember that what the physical practice looks like isn't important. What matters is how it feels to the person doing it and whether it effectively supports their physical, psychological, and spiritual health.

Yoga teachers should be sure not to neglect their own practice. It can be their best ally in maintaining the capacity to serve others. Be mindful that teaching yoga without refueling one's own tank by means of a personal practice results in less support for students and eventual burnout for the instructor. Don't just teach yoga. Also practice it, whether by oneself or in a group with others.

Even if teachers already have a strong yoga practice, engaging in other stress-reduction methods regularly is very helpful. What's most effective will vary greatly from person to person. Some suggestions: Get a massage, read for fun, take a digital detox, watch television, go to a movie, or talk to a friend. During more stressful, emotional times, allowing oneself to cry is a natural and important release.

Some individuals tend to let work (including service work) fill up their lives. For these yoga teachers, scheduling downtime to do something that reduces stress is essential.

Social Connection. One of the most important things we can do to take care of ourselves is to maintain a community of friends and family. Teachers should take the time to regularly connect with the people in their life who give them support. Knowing who can be counted on to listen and hold space when it is needed is invaluable.

Consider that connection goes beyond the people in our lives. Our relationships with pets can be particularly therapeutic. The same holds true for our relationship with all the animals, plants, waters, and rocks in nature. Taking time to notice and appreciate beauty in the natural world can be healing. Even a few seconds really looking at and appreciating a striking tree, flower, sunrise, or cloudscape can be meaningful and rejuvenating.

Be mindful that introverts and extroverts recharge differently. Although social connection is important for everyone, ongoing social interaction without breaks is typically draining and stressful for introverts. Such personalities should plan time to be alone so that they can connect with themselves and recharge.

Yoga service organizations should establish regular support group meetings for their teachers and staff. They might also consider creating social networking platforms and scheduling regular get-togethers to support social connection. If possible, teachers should debrief with a peer or supervisor soon after each service engagement.

Yoga teachers who are working on their own are encouraged to reach out to find others with whom they can connect who are doing similar work. If possible, instructors should connect with such colleagues in person on a regular basis. Online forums can also be set up that provide social support and connection with other yoga service teachers and organizations.

Secondary Trauma. It is crucial that yoga service providers and criminal justice professionals alike understand what secondary trauma is and how to recognize and proactively address it. Readers are encouraged to review the section "Proactively Address Secondary Trauma," detailed in chapter 2, and consult the relevant recommended resources listed in Appendix A.

RELATIONSHIP BUILDING:
PRACTICE CONSCIOUS RELATIONSHIP

Yoga services providers should practice conscious relationship, particularly in the teacher-student relationship.

The concept of "conscious relationship" is central to the Yoga Service Council's working definition of yoga service. Childress and Cohen Harper (2016) explain that:

> *Sharing yoga always takes place within the context of a relationship. A relationship involves many nuances of the human experience. Conscious relationship acknowledges these nuances and asks people to educate themselves about social justice issues (e.g., privilege, race, violence, gender, poverty) as well as to listen openly and with curiosity to each other's perspectives. To exist in a conscious relationship is to compassionately hold these truths about each other and about the world in our interactions. Conscious relationship is an active attempt to see each person fully, honor their strengths, and acknowledge anything that is impeding either person's ability to relate in full authenticity to the relationship. (p. 1)*

The ability to engage in conscious relationship is supported by the practice of self-inquiry. The more that we know ourselves—and are aware of the lens through which we see the others and the world—the more we can engage considerately and authentically with others.

Navigating Difference. In the context of the criminal justice system, issues pertaining to race, class, and gender differences become heightened. This can create a divisive environment. Left unacknowledged, these dynamics color perceptions and create obstacles to authentic relationships.

As much as possible, it's crucial to be aware of any preexisting biases that impact how we see ourselves and others. For yoga teachers, working first to become more aware of such lenses, and then to discard them in order to see ourselves and others more authentically, should be a core personal practice and resource for effective teaching.

Sharing common experiences can be a powerful component to a supportive relationship. However, it is not essential. Teachers should not try to mold themselves, their words, or their behaviors to match what they imagine their students will relate to on the basis of real or perceived differences. Presenting oneself in an inauthentic way only creates barriers to conscious relationship. If, however, shared experiences exist—for example, someone who was formerly incarcerated teaching in a facility themselves—appropriately acknowledging them is quite valuable.

"Unconditional Positive Regard." Practicing "unconditional positive regard" means accepting and respecting others as they are without judgment or evaluation. This is not to say that anyone has to like others or condone their behavior. Rather, it is a commitment to acknowledging their personal agency in choosing their actions, while also assuming that they are doing their best given their background and circumstances.

Cultivating this attitude forms the basis for creating an atmosphere that allows for a change in behavior. As Dr. Carl Rogers, the humanistic psychologist who proposed the concept of unconditional positive regard, says:

> the individual has within him or herself vast resources for self-understanding, for altering her or his self-concept, attitudes, and self-directed behavior—and that these resources can be tapped if only a definable climate of facilitative psychological attitudes can be provided.

For yoga teachers, meeting students with unconditional positive regard helps foster those "facilitative" attitudes that enable them to engage more effectively in processes of personal learning and growth (Rogers, 1986). This regard should be held for all people the yoga instructor encounters, whether incarcerated or staff.

> "Flexibility is everything in this work. There are classes where supporting community for many people is the goal and others where you may guide with only one or two students. There is opportunity for connection in all of it."

RELATIONSHIP BUILDING:
MAINTAIN PROFESSIONAL BOUNDARIES

The professional role of the yoga teacher should be clearly defined and its boundaries respected.

The job structure of yoga teachers in the criminal justice system varies widely. Some are individual volunteers with minimal supervision. Some are contractors with clearly specified expectations. Some are employees with job requirements and close supervision. Despite this variation, there are common guidelines that yoga teachers should follow in defining the boundaries of their professional role:

- **Follow Rules.** It is vital that yoga teachers know and follow institutional policies and procedures without exception. Volunteers must remember that they are guests of their institution or agency, even if that entity relies on volunteers to carry out essential functions of the programming offered. Contractors and employees should remember that they have been contracted to fulfill a specific role and be conscientious about not overstepping it.

Yoga teachers should understand that system staff may at times need to be appropriately firm and commanding with students. Instructors should keep in mind that they may not understand the full context, as they can't know what's happening during the 23 hours of the day they're not there.

Even if teachers witness what appears to be negative treatment or lack of respect from staff, it is beyond their professional role to contradict staff publicly. If teachers believe there is an abuse issue that should be addressed, they should follow the proper chain of command within their organization and the institution to address the situation.

- **Communicate Effectively.** A large part of professionalism is honoring one's commitments. Yoga teachers are responsible to be direct and transparent in communicating anything that might get in the way of their ability to do so, whether due to personal, organizational, or institutional issues.

  Teachers are also encouraged to regularly ask for feedback from appropriate people in the institution they're serving. Demonstrating that institutional input is valued helps strengthen relationships and may generate important information that can bolster yoga programming.

- **Avoid Personal Relationships.** It is not appropriate for yoga teachers to develop personal relationships with students or staff. Any relationship that goes beyond a professional role has the potential to create confusion and codependency. Even if the intention is to help, the impact may be an erosion of personal agency. It may also lead to disappointment, anger, or resentment if (and most likely, when) teachers fail to fulfill expectations that exceed their professional capacity. Inappropriate personal relationships may also create a divisive "us" versus "them" mentality or create the impression of unfair favoritism.

  Sexual relationships in a prison environment are strictly forbidden. Power dynamics in this context confuse considerations of consent in ways that cannot be untangled.

- **Limit Personal Disclosure.** Teachers should strictly limit disclosure of personal information to that which is relevant to the practice and in service of their students. Sharing how yoga has helped one's personal life may be relevant. For instance, teachers might share if they have personally used yoga in overcoming addictions or managing anger. Sharing information about personal relationships, living situation, and other aspects of everyday life is not relevant and should be avoided.

Yoga service providers should understand that personal information can be a highly valuable commodity in a prison or jail setting. Potentially, it could be leveraged to intimidate or blackmail. Even if the information seems innocuous, teachers must remain vigilant about sharing only that which is directly relevant to yoga instruction.

By the same token, they must protect others by respecting the confidentiality of any personal disclosures made by students or staff, and by being careful about discussing any person or group around others. Service providers should also do what they can to limit such disclosures. For example, if students choose to share information about why they are involved with the criminal justice system, teachers should not ask for details.

> "Sharing inappropriate personal information may create envy and distance students. For example, one of our teachers told incarcerated youth that she taught her father yoga, and, even though he initially thought it was for girls, he ended up loving it. I noticed the boys go numb. Perhaps many of them don't have fathers in their lives or have difficult relationships with them. We don't know."

- **Make Referrals.** Mindful yoga practice can bring emotions, memories, and traumas stored deep in the body up to the surface of everyday consciousness. Such psychoemotional dynamics are valuable in that they open the possibility of practicing yoga in ways that are healing and empowering not simply physically but holistically.

  That said, yoga teachers are not counselors or therapists, and should never step into these roles. Given that feelings and issues may come up for students that they need additional support to integrate, teachers should be ready to refer them to appropriate mental health professionals, if possible. If such resources are not available, teachers should consider how best to recalibrate classes to protect students from opening up too many feelings too quickly.

- **Say "No" When Appropriate.** Teachers should be aware that their students, yoga service organization, other teachers, or the institution they're serving may ask them to give more than they are capable of or comfortable with. For example, teachers might be asked to do "favors" that violate facility policy, teach more classes than they can handle, or provide services beyond their scope of practice. To maintain appropriate boundaries, they must be ready to refuse such requests.

  Teachers may encounter students who attempt to use manipulation, coercion, or blackmail to push them beyond their limits. Small "favors," for example, can escalate and create serious problems. Establishing clear boundaries early in the relationship can help avoid such situations. If teachers transgress an institutional policy, no matter how small, they must immediately self-report it to the appropriate authority to prevent the situation from growing beyond their ability to contain.

- **Separate Yoga and Politics.** Yoga teachers should not attempt to play a role in changing the political environment or the institution they're serving that extends beyond that of providing quality yoga programming. Of course, individuals involved in this work may (and arguably should) have additional roles as citizens beyond this purview. The role of the yoga teacher, however, should maintain its unique integrity.

Teachers may be justifiably upset by the injustices they learn about or encounter directly in the system. However, it is more productive for yoga service leaders to have a "seat at the table" with key decision makers in the system than to alienate them. Building good relationships between yoga service providers and criminal justice professionals supports system-involved individuals who wish to learn yoga and experience its benefits. Over time, greater acceptance of the healing capacities of yoga will ideally help leverage policy-level changes in the system, particularly around issues of trauma sensitivity and physical and mental health.

RELATIONSHIP BUILDING: EDUCATE STAFF

Yoga service providers should educate staff at all levels regarding how and why their program benefits students and the institution.

Many people have mistaken or incomplete perceptions about yoga. Communicating the benefits of a trauma-informed yoga practice can help reshape those perceptions and win greater support for yoga in the system. Yoga service providers should be able to explain not only the content of class offerings but what outcomes they hope to achieve and why these goals are realistic. Such explanations are particularly effective when presented in clear language backed up by scientific theory and research. Ideally, organizations will have printed material available such as a brochure or one-page handout that delivers their core message succinctly.

It's important that yoga providers consider how best to communicate with different occupational groups in the system such as administrative staff, custody staff, health care providers, and mental health workers. Support for quality yoga instruction will increase to the extent that such stakeholders understand why having it available might support them in the course of their everyday work.

Health care workers, mental health providers, social workers, and recreational therapists are most likely to be aware of the growing body of evidence supporting yoga and mindfulness as complementary health and wellness practices. While this means that they may be the greatest allies of yoga programming, their support should never be assumed or taken for granted. Yoga service providers should seek to understand their perspective and objectives, and work with them as partners to grow the acceptance of yoga and mindfulness in the institution.

Understand Staff Concerns. Yoga providers should be aware that there may be conflicting responses to the addition of outside programming among different staff in a facility. Administration and volunteer services may be positive about the presence of yoga programming; custody staff may be less enthusiastic. This makes sense in that the primary role of custody is to maintain safety for all parties involved. The added presence of yoga teachers and programs increases their workload and responsibilities. Yoga teachers are wise to understand such dynamics and strive to be respectful, supportive, authentic, and nonjudgmental.

> "It took six years, but consistently demonstrating the positive impact of our program eventually built trust and respect with corrections staff. We are now allowed to bring in blankets, blocks, handouts, and books."

RELATIONSHIP BUILDING:
OFFER YOGA INSTRUCTION TO STAFF

Yoga service providers should offer yoga and mindfulness instruction to correctional officers and other staff.

One of the best ways to gain greater acceptance for bringing yoga into the criminal justice system is to find ways to offer the benefits of the practice to staff. If they have the capacity, yoga service providers should arrange to attend one or more staff meetings in which they can introduce yoga techniques to help staff manage their stress. In facilities where there is sufficent acceptance and support, it is ideal to establish ongoing classes for staff. Alternatively, yoga providers can work with local studios to offer free trials and discounted memberships for them.

There is no question that the stress-reducing and health-enhancing benefits of yoga are sorely needed among correctional officers and other frontline staff. One 2013 study estimated that 31 percent of U.S. correctional officers suffer from PTSD, more than four times the national average and on a par with veterans returning from war. Other studies show significantly reduced life expectancy due to stress-related health issues, as well as a suicide rate 39 percent higher than the national average (Lopez, 2014). Supporting staff in managing their stress not only benefits them as individuals but also their families, coworkers, those they are charged with supervising, and the facility and surrounding community as a whole.

RELATIONSHIP BUILDING: SUPPORT THE FIELD

Yoga service providers should understand and take responsibility for the fact that they are part of a new and growing field of service.

To offer yoga in the criminal justice system is to be part of a new and growing field of service. Greater public and professional awareness of the impact of trauma, particularly traumatic events experienced in childhood, along with new research supporting yoga and mindfulness as a path to recovery, has opened the door to greater acceptance of these practices. This is an unprecedented situation. Even a decade ago, these conditions didn't exist, and system-supported yoga programs were quite rare.

The growth of this new field presents yoga service providers with both opportunity and responsibility. Those who are becoming newly involved should remember that the hard work, dedication, and professionalism of others who preceded them succeeded in opening doors. How yoga teachers and organizations engage with the system today can pave the way for even greater acceptance of these practices for others in the future.

As the field grows and matures, there are expanding opportunities to work with others doing this work and to join or form an organization. There are new opportunities for organizations to develop relationships with one another and share resources, knowledge, and experience. The more that such collaboration occurs, the more this field of service is strengthened. For example, this collection of best practices is a direct result of relationships formed through conscious collaboration in a spirit of generosity from the contributing individuals and organizations involved.

RELATIONSHIP BUILDING:
DEVELOP COMPLEMENTARY PARTNERSHIPS

Yoga service organizations should develop partnerships with groups and organizations doing complementary work within the system and at the community, state, and national levels.

Yoga cannot offer a complete solution to the challenges faced by system-involved people. Many other groups are doing complementary work that could be fruitfully connected to yoga. Housing and workforce development programs, for instance, can benefit from integrating a wellness and mindfulness component. Meditation, art therapy, and writing classes are another natural fit.

Connecting with such groups can create opportunities for developing more-comprehensive resources that help meet the broader needs of people involved in the system. The more that the yoga service field can become integrated into a broadening array of human services and supports, the more it will positively impact individuals, institutions, and communities.

Yoga service organizations can connect with prospective partners by participating in relevant legislative hearings, becoming involved with coalitions, and attending criminal justice–related events. Funders and major supporters may be able to suggest particular individuals and groups to connect with, as well as provide access to the forums where these connections can be made.

RELATIONSHIP BUILDING:
EDUCATE COMMUNITY STAKEHOLDERS

Yoga service providers should seek to educate community stakeholders on how yoga can benefit system-involved people.

Like people working within the system, community stakeholders may have mistaken or incomplete perceptions about yoga. Consequently, they may not see why they might want to support a given yoga service organization or yoga in the criminal justice system more generally.

Yoga service organizations can lay the groundwork for positive relationships with such individuals and organizations by first seeking to understand their relationship to the criminal justice system and the outcomes they hope to foster. Then, any presentation of how yoga might be valuable can be tailored to maximize its relevance to the stakeholder's interests.

Examples of stakeholders in the community are unlimited. Since the criminal justice system is funded by tax dollars, every tax-paying citizen has a stake. Yoga service providers should be prepared to encounter negative pushback from community members who reject the goal of providing yoga to system-involved people. The more that yoga teachers and organizations are well informed about the system (both locally and nationally) and can clearly communicate why yoga can be beneficial, the more they can increase public awareness of the realities—as opposed to stereotypes surrounding the system—and perhaps generate greater compassion for those involved.

Although everyone has a stake, yoga service providers should consider focusing their efforts on educating stakeholders who are likely to have some influence on policy, offer financial support, or be willing to partner as a provider of complementary services or programming. Examples include legislatures, judges, attorneys, probation and parole offices, law enforcement, victims' rights organizations, reentry programs, health service providers, victim's rights organizations, housing agencies, workforce training, educational assistance, veteran's groups, faith-based organizations, and so on (CEPP, 2015).

5

ORGANIZATIONAL DEVELOPMENT

Offering yoga in the criminal justice system in ways that are safe, effective, healing, trauma-informed, and culturally responsive is very demanding work. As such, it is ideally supported by strong, sustainable yoga service organizations with excellent teacher selection, training, mentoring, and supervisory processes.

Developing such an organization, however, is an exceptionally demanding endeavor in and of itself. This chapter provides interested readers with an overview of how to launch, build, and develop a high-quality yoga service organization that's capable of doing this work. Based on the collective firsthand experience and knowledge of leaders in the field who have gone through this process themselves, this chapter offers uniquely valuable insights into the organizational development process.

The discussion of yoga service organizational development proceeds from aspiring start-up through DOC system approval and ongoing program development. For a simplified typology of different stages of organizational development, ranging from "Start-Up" to "Growing," "Established," and "Mature," see Appendix B.

ORGANIZATIONAL DEVELOPMENT: DEVELOP A PLAN

Yoga service providers should clarify their intention and assess the level of commitment needed to make their program or class a success.

Aspiring yoga service providers are advised to take the time to develop a solid plan regarding what they wish to accomplish and what this will likely require. The complexity of such a start-up plan will vary according to whether a program or class is new or part of an established organization; structured as a for-profit or nonprofit; and the level of resources available. Key elements of a good start-up plan include:

1. Short- and long-term objectives and goals

2. Fundraising/revenue strategy

3. Strategic plan/business plan

4. Analysis of the relevant institutional/human ecosystem

The process of developing these core elements can be aided by considering the following questions:

Who do I want to teach? Although there are overarching commonalities, different populations require different considerations in terms of yoga instruction, teaching staff, and class environment. Examples of different populations that could be focused on include:

- Men and/or women in jail or prison (special populations include people who are pregnant, veterans, on mental health units, and/or 55 or older)

- Incarcerated teenage girls and/or boys

- Youth, women or men in alternative schools, work-release programs, halfway homes, or residential treatment facilities

- People on probation

- Correctional officers

What's my mission and vision? Crafting a formal mission and vision statement is a good way to clarify one's thoughts and communicate goals to others. It's okay to start simple; these statements can and should be refined as the work evolves. Having a clear sense of the intended impact will anchor the work and provide a powerful framework within which to craft a business plan, class curriculum, and strategy for approaching facilities.

Who's needed on my team? Based on the scope of the envisioned program, decide what skills are needed for yoga teaching, administrative work, fundraising, and organizational development. Again, starting small is fine. Once a solid foundation is established, the program can build as needed over time.

Be aware that administrative tasks usually take significantly longer than initially imagined. Also, be mindful that setting programs up in ways that demand a huge input of time and energy for little or no compensation will likely prove unsustainable over time. Avoiding burnout is a serious challenge in all social service fields, and yoga is no exception. Strive to keep the time commitments required of yourself and others to a sustainable level, even if that means beginning with a less ambitious program than you might ideally like.

> "Having a clearly stated mission, vision, and core values has helped us avoid dilution of our work or becoming 'spread too thin.' These are our 'polestars' guiding us to make decisions each and every day, a key piece of sustainability for an organization."

What benefits will my program offer? While the curriculum will likely evolve with time, it's best to launch a class or program with a well thought-out class plan linked to clearly stated objectives. Be ready to describe the intended impacts of what is being offered to class participants, facility staff, and other stakeholders in language that is meaningful and accessible to them.

What's my program name? Choose a program name that can be easily understood and pronounced, and that clearly reflects the work being done. Make the language inviting—help people understand what the class or program is about. Be aware that using Sanskrit may create barriers to acceptance. Similarly, yoga service providers should be mindful that using words that label the population they seek to serve might be perceived as stigmatizing, offensive, or otherwise off-putting (e.g., "Gangster Yoga"). When considering names, perform a thorough online search to ensure that no one has already selected it or something highly similar. This is important both to avoid copyright issues and potential confusion about organizational boundaries.

ORGANIZATIONAL DEVELOPMENT: RESEARCH POTENTIAL PROGRAM SITES

Yoga service providers should thoroughly research potential program sites to determine whether they may be a good fit and how best to approach them.

Before approaching any facility or other potential program site, it's critical to conduct background research to determine whether it's a good fit and, if so, how yoga service providers might gain entry. Key points to consider when researching potential sites include:

Commuting Requirements. Think realistically about the time commitment required to get to and from the site. Many facilities are located in remote areas. Those in urban centers may be time consuming to access during rush hours. Be aware that commute time can become a source of burnout for teachers.

Population Demographics. Basic information about potential program sites can often be found on the Internet. The Department of Corrections requires facilities to provide annual "report cards" that provide information on numbers of people incarcerated, demographics, and so forth.

Potential Contacts and Allies. The best way to get a class or program started and keep it running smoothly is to develop relationships with site employees who support it personally and are in a position to make a difference institutionally. Yoga teachers and program staff should develop their networking skills to identify potential contacts and follow up on any leads diligently.

Once good contacts have been identified, yoga service providers should be thoughtful about what will help build and maintain these relationships further. Teachers are wise to keep in mind that their credibility will be enhanced considerably when it's evident that they have learned as much about the site as they reasonably can—and that they have a clear sense of what will be offered and why it will be beneficial.

Providers should be prepared for the lengthy time (sometimes years) it may take to gain access to a facility. They should remain tenacious and kind. Sooner or later, a connection with people who support the proposed program will be made, and this connection can help cut through any red tape.

Even yoga service providers who are doing everything right might still experience a facility saying "no." Of course, this can be discouraging. Time-tested experience, however, demonstrates that often doors *will* open over time.

Other Organizational Players. Many facilities list nonprofit and religious organizations that offer programs at their location. It's worth taking the time to speak with knowledgeable individuals from these organizations, as even if their program has nothing to do with yoga, they may have invaluable advice regarding how best to approach the site (suggested contacts, protocols, etc.).

As mentioned, Departments of Corrections can be complex institutions into which to bring yoga services. Often, administrative personnel are already managing the maximum number of relationships and programs they can handle. Internal resources such as staffing, time, and classrooms may be over-allocated. In such cases, partnering with an existing organization that is already delivering programs may be a service provider's best bet. If a good fit, joining forces with an existing provider has the added benefits of supporting collaboration in the field and avoiding duplication of services.

ORGANIZATIONAL DEVELOPMENT: ASSESS PROGRAM AND ORGANIZATIONAL NEEDS

Yoga service providers should determine their specific role in the program or organization and who else might be needed to meet its objectives.

Based on the scope of the envisioned program, yoga service providers need to assess who and what they'll need to make it successful. Key elements of an assessment process include:

Self-Assessment. Leaders should engage in self-inquiry to identify their highest and best fit with the intended class, program, and/or organization. Questions to reflect seriously on include:

- What am I good at? What am I willing to learn?

- How might I get in the way of my program reaching its highest potential?

- Is my greatest joy teaching yoga? Am I interested and ready to take on administrative duties that come with managing an organization?

- Am I good at scheduling and handling logistics? Or do I need to find others with these skill sets?

Determine Needs. Once leaders have assessed the scope of their own intended roles, they can better determine what they will need from others. They should be specific, asking questions such as: Do I need five yoga instructors who are well versed in working with youth? Do I need someone to develop a website for me? How am I going to sustain my efforts? Where will my funding come from?

If yoga service providers are thinking of forming a nonprofit, be sure to consider how this would impact organizational structure. For example, it will be necessary to develop a board of directors. Ideally, the board would include people with different relevant skill sets such as law, finance, fundraising, communications, and so on. Often, it's helpful to establish an advisory board to provide the new organization with additional support, credibility, and expertise.

If possible, both the board of directors and the advisory board would include representatives from the targeted population, so that their voices can be integrated in the work being done. For instance, if the plan is to work with youth, teachers should consider a few youth advisors (ideally former program participants).

Build a Core Team. Although it may sound easier to "go it alone" at first, sharing the responsibility of the program creates stability and sustainability. Find others who can be part of the start-up efforts, even if it's a small group of three dedicated teachers. Whether the intention is to offer one class a week at one facility, or create a nonprofit with multiple program sites, it's critical to assemble a (small) team of people to prevent burnout and ensure consistency of the class or program.

Develop Teachers. It's a good idea for yoga service providers to have an idea of how to approach mentorship and training for yoga teachers who join the program. Providers should strive to create loyalty in the team by being transparent, organized, and reliable. A good goal is to have people in training at all times—life happens, and there will be turnover.

Build Connections. Even before the program starts, service providers are wise to start building relationships within the facility or program site to educate, collect feedback, and cultivate allies. Finding advocates and champions within the facility on all levels can take years but is invaluable. Providers should attend volunteer-appreciation events, fairs, and other gatherings hosted by the facility to build a network.

Yoga service providers may want to reach out to people who are current or past employees of the criminal justice system and solicit their advice and support. Promising avenues for making these important connections include:

- Attending events centered around criminal justice in the targeted community

- Asking other organizations working within the system to make an introduction (see above, do research)

- Hosting a roundtable where people can share feedback and advice

- Being prepared to give presentations when requested. Groups, entities, and events such as the Rotary Club, Juvenile Justice Conference, Center for Health Justice, and Department of Children and Family Services will likely be interested. They may ask yoga service providers to participate as the work becomes more established and well known.

Think Beyond Your Own Tenure. Leaders are encouraged to document their organization's processes and structures so that others within it can easily understand how it works. It's important to develop a succession plan so that a program or organization has life beyond its founders and nurtures the next generation of potential leaders.

ORGANIZATIONAL DEVELOPMENT: CRAFT CURRICULUM

Yoga service organizations and individual teachers should craft a curriculum that best meets the needs of the population served.

Yoga service providers are advised to craft a clear curriculum that offers continuity among different teachers, makes the work replicable, and grounds classes in a larger framework. Having a curriculum makes the work significantly more intentional and consistent, and helps improve the overall quality of the class or program. (For a detailed discussion of curriculum considerations, see chapter 3, "Curriculum and Instruction.")

Curricula vary from program to program and may be more or less detailed. At first, the curriculum may simply be an outline of the yoga class and its intended outcomes. From there, it can be refined and expanded over time. Teachers should review the curriculum regularly and integrate any new "on the ground" experiences, along with any new knowledge gained regarding best practices in the field.

When developing a curriculum, it's important to link content to specific intended outcomes. Ideally, these should be both short and long term. For example, instructors might ask, What will students have experienced after one class? After six weeks?

Service providers should create a program proposal based on a four-, six-, or eight-week cycle, rather than for an undefined period of time. Program cycles are easier to fund, and a specific curriculum can be developed based on the number of classes.

It's important to be aware that funders generally request clearly specified objectives and outcomes. Any evaluation that can be done to measure success will not only help refine the work but give it credibility with funders and other professionals interested in the effectiveness of the program.

ORGANIZATIONAL DEVELOPMENT: PREPARE A PITCH

Yoga service providers should prepare a pitch to a potential program site tailored to speak to the concerns and priorities of the audience.

Once yoga organizations or individual teachers have succeeded in connecting with a potential program site, it's time to present the proposal. To prepare for the meeting, they should craft a message that can be understood by a non-yoga audience. Presenters might ask themselves, Will I be speaking with the mental health staff? Recreation? Upper-level administration? The presentation should be tailored to the particular audience, while remaining truthful to what the program has to offer. The program needs to be explained in ways that will be meaningful to people who've never heard of trauma-informed yoga. Presenters should be concise and professional, and seek to create connection and common ground.

Yoga service providers are advised to consider developing a one-page "sell sheet" detailing the proven benefits of yoga and meditation. The mission of the program, its intended benefits, and relevant research citations should be included. Remember that a facility may have different priorities than those of yoga service providers. Therefore, yoga organizations and individual teachers are encouraged to look for alignment and shared values (such as safety), and then be able to speak specifically to related needs and goals.

There also may be concerns about how the program might be perceived by the public. Yoga service providers should have a ready response to comments like: "What, free yoga for convicts? No way!" Providers must be sensitive to the fact that yoga programs for incarcerated people may trigger resentments among those who see themselves as put-upon taxpayers who can't afford such "luxuries" themselves.

Ask Questions. Although the primary purpose of a pitch meeting is to explain the benefit of the program, it's also a vital opportunity to learn more about the potential program site. Questions to consider asking when interfacing with the facility include:

- If the program is accepted, who will my primary contacts be? What is the best way to work with them?

- What other classes or programs are available at the facility, both in general and at the time I would be offering my class? Would my class be part of a larger curriculum or set of programs that students have to complete? If so, is it possible to review how my program is folded into this overarching curriculum?

- Are there options regarding what category or department my program might be housed in (e.g., religion, recreation, health and wellness, therapy)? If so, what are the implications of different options (where classes would be held, etc.)? (If the program is grouped under religious programming, understand the implications of this—some potential students may not come out of fear that yoga will conflict with their faith.)

- Is there a budget available to support this program?

- Are there any restrictions or recommendations regarding how I might publicly discuss or advertise my program?

- Would it be possible to attend a staff meeting in order to learn more about the facility and, if possible, briefly introduce my program? Could I offer staff a sample class or short demo session (e.g., a 10-minute chair yoga session)?

Program leaders and yoga teachers should also make sure that they also know the answers to basic questions concerning class logistics:

- What would the classroom look like and what kind of yoga props would be allowed?

- How will students be recruited and vetted for the program? Would classes be mandatory or voluntary? Would it be a privilege for students to attend?

- Would students sign up for a session (e.g., four to six weeks) or will classes be offered on a drop-in/rolling basis?

- Does the facility record class attendance? If so, who is responsible? What method is used?

- (For youth classes only) Will students get PE credit or any other high school credit for participation in the program?

ORGANIZATIONAL DEVELOPMENT: BUILD INFRASTRUCTURE

Developing infrastructure that supports program quality and sustainability is essential.

Once yoga service providers receive permission to offer yoga instruction, they should take a moment to celebrate! This is a big accomplishment. Be aware, however, that it's also usually only the beginning of a long logistical process. The facility may have many time-consuming requirements to meet, including trainings, clearance procedures, and a lengthy approval processes for any materials you wish to bring in (e.g., mats and yoga props). Providers should not give up! Future students will thank them. This is an excellent opportunity to practice patience and flexibility.

This is also a point at which it's critical for program leaders to review whether they have the infrastructure needed to maintain the fidelity of their programs. If not, they would be wise to build it out as expeditiously as possible. Depending on the scope of the program, the following elements may be necessary:

- Written policies, procedures, and safety protocols

- Job descriptions for instructors

- Code of conduct for instructors while teaching (e.g., clear instructions on how to work with students and staff, both normally and when faced with challenging situations)

- Dress code for teachers

- Social media policy for teachers and staff

- Simple program-evaluation protocol (see the "Document and Evaluate" section later in this chapter)

Teachers must understand facility and/or unit rules, as well as how staff supervision of their classes will work. There should be a plan for how to communicate this information to them, as well as to any program volunteers or staff.

As discussed previously, there must *always* be a staff member present in the room for youth classes. Staff presence is also preferred for adult classes but is not absolutely required as with youth. Remember that safety is often a facility's primary concern and that staff may see people coming in from the outside to offer programs as a liability.

ORGANIZATIONAL DEVELOPMENT: SEEK DIVERSIFIED FUNDING

Yoga services providers should seek to develop a diversified funding base so that teachers and core staff can be compensated.

Offering classes free of charge for a predetermined pilot period is an excellent means of gaining access and getting started. Once that's complete, it's best to receive compensation from the facility/program site for services, if feasible. If yoga is offered for free for an indefinite, open-ended period of time, it will be difficult to shift to being paid. This is to be avoided, if possible.

That said, many facilities cannot or will not fund yoga programs. In such cases, cultivating alternative sources of funding should be a top priority.

Receiving payment for yoga services is important because it helps support the quality, consistency, and sustainability of the program—and, by extension, of the yoga service field more generally. Yoga service organizations have a responsibility to hire highly qualified teachers who have the training and maturity necessary to work with students with high rates of trauma in an often challenging and unpredictable setting. Paying teachers enables organizations to be more selective, demand greater accountability, and reduce burnout. Although many people in this field are passionate about their work and would be willing to do it without pay, over time this typically proves unsustainable. It is also important to recognize that this is real work that deserves real compensation.

Money Matters. Program leaders and yoga teachers are encouraged to take time to reflect on their assumptions and knowledge about money, around both psychological issues of power and worthiness, and concrete matters of budgeting, fundraising, and financial literacy. When looking deeply into their own relationships to this often highly charged issue, yoga service providers can ask themselves: What are my blind spots? What are my strengths? What do I need to learn? What blockages might I need to get past?

It is critical that program leaders and individual teachers educate themselves on the practical and psychological dynamics of money. If they aren't comfortable asking for financial support, they might take action to address their internal blocks and learn this skill set. They can consider investing in an online and/or in-person training if necessary. The Foundation Center offers many resources. These and other materials can be easily located with an online search.

If leaders know that they are lacking certain skill sets or capabilities around money matters, they can consider adding someone to their team who can assist them.

Of course, it's imperative to raise funds ethically to uphold the integrity of both the program and the field. Program leaders should be familiar with codes of conduct and national standards around fundraising and soliciting money, such as provided by the Association of Fundraising Professionals. When receiving a financial gift or grant, they should follow best practices of accountability to their funders.

Calculating Costs. Yoga service providers need to get specific about the costs of their program. Setting up and maintaining a weekly yoga class involves expenses beyond the initial purchase of mats and other supplies. For example, teachers will be spending money traveling to the site. In some locales, these costs can be substantial. There may also be administrative expenses, curricular development costs, and teacher fees (e.g., liability insurance).

Once costs have been ascertained, organizations and individual teachers are advised to calculate the market value of the services provided. For example, they should assess how much administrative, teaching, and commuting time is being accrued, and then assign value to it based on a reasonable estimation of what the relevant hourly wages would be if these positions were fully funded. Then, when asking for funding, they should compare the amount requested to this market-based cost estimate. Typically, what is being requested will be substantially less than this number. Make that cost savings explicit in any conversations exploring contracts, grants, or other potential funding.

Public Funding. If yoga classes are to be offered in a correctional facility, it is best to explore the possibility of contracting for services before beginning a free pilot session. Program leaders should be clear on how the program can benefit the facility. For example, if the facility becomes safer, this produces cost savings in terms of staff time. Although the benefits of yoga instruction are obviously much bigger, appealing to a facility's bottom line generally helps leverage success in such conversations. Providers should be confident in the projected outcomes of their programs so that they can ask for compensation assertively.

Most correctional facilities have what's commonly called an "inmate canteen fund." Here, a percentage of the profits from the sale of canteen items to incarcerated people is directed to a fund for programmatic/recreation purposes (e.g., purchasing basketballs). Where available, these monies might be one source of internal public funding. Other sources may be available as well. Providers are encouraged to research options and speak to sympathetic, knowledgeable insiders as much as possible. Keep in mind, however, that many, if not most facilities may not have money available.

The funding landscape varies from jurisdiction to jurisdiction, as well as from agency to agency, service area to service area, and among populations served. Program leaders should understand the budget cycles within their jurisdictions: Money to pay for their work may be allocated already. They can start by looking at their city or county website, and learning more about the budgeting process. They can try to find a council member or aide who might be willing to speak with them. They can also try to learn more about grants that could contain elements that are relevant to their work, such as a juvenile block grant or crime-prevention grant, and how and when to apply for them.

Sometimes the government puts out RFPs (requests for proposals) or RFQs (requests for qualifications). Being included in these notifications requires being a "squeaky wheel." Yoga service providers can call the probation analyst or other relevant official and ask to be included on the notification list when funding becomes available for contracted services.

Once there is a contract with county government, program leaders will be notified when it is up for renewal. Even so, providers shouldn't take any arrangement for granted. It remains really important to maintain a connection with whoever is handling these processes (which could change regularly and may include more than one person).

Other Options. Yoga service providers are wise to aim to diversify their funding base. Being creative can prove fruitful. Program leaders should explore a wide range of options such as family foundations, community foundations, corporate foundations, local businesses, charity auctions, donation classes, and more. Potential partnerships with other organizations that could make the work more efficient and effective is another good consideration.

Service providers should be wary of "event heavy" fundraising strategies that require putting a lot of time and effort into small events that may not raise very much money. They should keep in mind the investment of time and resources in relationship to the fundraising goal. Is the investment of hours worth the financial return? If not, they may not elect to do it.

If yoga service organizations are not able to find sufficient funding to pay teachers, they can consider other means of supporting them such as mileage reimbursement or free continuing education.

ORGANIZATIONAL DEVELOPMENT: CONSIDER ORGANIZATIONAL STRUCTURE CAREFULLY

Yoga service providers must consider what sort of organizational structure is needed, and build it systematically over time.

Even if a yoga service program is just starting out, it's helpful to envision what a more highly developed organization might look like so that leaders can lay the foundation for it gradually. Often, yoga service organizations are founded by the hard work of one person, and thereby have a hard time developing a more integrated structure. Program leaders should think proactively about how to supervise, train, and support teachers and staff so that they become increasingly knowledgeable and well integrated into the organization. As it grows, seeking to build a strong leadership team so that everything isn't reliant on one person is prudent. Eventually, the organization should be able to continue on strongly, even without the original founder at the helm.

"Scaffold" Supervision and Support. Working toward a "scaffolded" organizational structure that sorts teachers and staff into several differentiated tiers of experience and expertise is an important consideration. Organizations should set up each tier so that those in it can provide supervision, training, and support to those in the tier below.

A concrete example of this would be that new teachers first participate in a class taught by an experienced teacher.[13] Then, when they are more familiar with the class, they can move up to assist them. This allows new teachers to both experience and informally demonstrate poses as they are taught. It also allows students to get used to a teacher-in-training, while lessening their sense of "being watched" by an unknown newcomer. Assistant teaching can then begin on a more comfortable basis for all concerned.

Ideally, this process will be further supported by formal opportunities for pre- and post-debriefing between the experienced and in-training teacher. Such setups support the former by providing a well-trained assistant and the latter by providing professional development and mentoring. (See also chapter 2, "Training and Staffing.")

By extending the scaffolding structure upward, experienced teachers should have opportunities to move into leadership roles that contribute to organizational development. Building such professional connections and developmental

---

13 In keeping with trauma-informed principles, it is crucial that new teachers in such scenarios participate in class actively rather than simply observe. Being watched tends to severely undercut students' sense of safety, predictability, and control, which together are a necessary foundation for trauma-informed yoga.

trajectories into the organization from the outset will contribute to its long-term sustainability, as everything won't be structured around the skills and charisma of one individual at the top. It creates an integrated structure through which the organization can grow without overloading capacity and creating burnout. Such a leadership model supports consistency, cohesiveness, stability, fidelity to the program, and reliability for participants and systems.

Consider Expansion Carefully. Program leaders should work closely with other senior members of their team to carefully consider the pros and cons of any proposed program expansion. Keep in mind that if the scope of work is expanded, program leaders who love to teach yoga may need to move into a more administrative role—and this can be challenging.

All leaders are encouraged to have regular self-check-ins in order to stay aligned with their passions and mission. They should be realistic about their own capacity and that of the organization, and stay focused on the needs of those they are serving.

If providers are operating a multisite program, there may be times when it's necessary to scale down or terminate programming at one site (particularly one that hasn't been successful) in order to sustain the resources at others. Resist the temptation to sacrifice the quality of the offerings to maintain some arbitrary target in terms of numbers served. Prioritize organizational integrity over size and growth.

Founder's Syndrome. "Founder's syndrome" is a well-known term in the non-profit and business worlds. It refers to the problems that develop when an organization has outgrown the stage where everything is centered around the founder, yet the structure hasn't shifted to reflect that. Instead, the founder maintains an excessive degree of centralized control, which creates bottlenecks, inefficiencies, and other dysfunctions, while underutilizing and alienating staff.

It is imperative that program leaders understand what "founder's syndrome" is and how to detect it. A lot of information is available online. Leaders are encouraged to think about how they can be proactive in heading this problem off at the pass. They should be intentional about building an organization that has the capacity to outlive their tenure with it.

Program leaders should study with others who have been in the field for many years. They can learn from others' mistakes and successes to build their own programs. They might attend online or in-person trainings, research websites, ask for help, and admit their blind spots. Building relationships with other organizations doing similar work (not necessarily yoga-based) is a vital means of developing allies and networks, and generating knowledge and understanding.

Organizations may outgrow their founder's individual capacities and skill set. If and when that happens, founders should be ready to see that as something to celebrate!

ORGANIZATIONAL DEVELOPMENT: DOCUMENT AND EVALUATE

Yoga service providers should establish procedures to document work and evaluate the program regularly.

Start-up programs are often so focused on the challenges of getting their classes up and running that little to no attention is paid to documenting the work. By the same token, there is often no advance thought given to the critically important question of how the program will be evaluated. Yoga service providers are wise to avoid these common mistakes. It is essential to document what a program is doing so that a solid case can be made to potential funders for support and to accurately assess what is going well and where there is room for improvement.

Data Collection. First, it's critical to collect hard data (i.e., reliable numbers). This doesn't have to be anything complicated. It does, however, need to supply meaningful information and be consistently and reliably generated. Yoga service providers should take the time necessary to set up and refine documentation systems from the get-go. They should not wait until the program is more highly developed—it will be impossible to capture what's been done in the past once it's over.

Collecting the following basic data from the inception of the program is prudent:

- Number of people served

- Demographics of people served (e.g., gender, age, etc.)

- Length of class

- Number of classes

- Any additional workshops or presentations

- Total number of service hours

It is essential to educate teachers, staff, and volunteers on the importance of data collection. They will not necessarily appreciate why it is important unless it is explained to them. Data collection systems should be set up so that they are as easy to manage as possible. Yoga service providers should think into how best to streamline and integrate relevant information streams.

Any data collection conducted while working under the purview of the criminal justice system requires prior approval from the point of contact. In advance, if possible, yoga service providers should discuss what numbers they hope to collect and see if there are any existing protocols in place that they could piggyback onto. They can check with more well-established organizations doing similar work (not necessarily yoga related) to see what has and hasn't worked well for them. While the numbers may not seem important or impressive at the outset, they accrue quickly and provide a vital record of the work that cannot be replicated later.

Program Evaluation. Start-up organizations are often intimidated by the thought of program evaluation—and avoid it as a result. Yoga service providers should not make this common mistake. Program evaluations can be simple but important and effective nevertheless. As the organization develops, program leaders should review their evaluation protocols and refine them as necessary to reflect what they've learned about the process itself and how the organization has developed.

Program leaders are advised to familiarize themselves with the basic concept of program evaluation, if it is foreign to them. There are many resources available online. They need to keep in mind that while program evaluations can get very complex, for a start-up or small program it's appropriate to keep it simple and easily doable. Whatever numbers are collected should be integrated into the program evaluation. The process might also collect more descriptive, in-depth information periodically (ideally, biannually or annually).

The program evaluation should collect data on core program objectives translated into measurable terms. This involves several steps:

1. **Identify the internal organizational dynamics that need to be assessed.** For example, check whether the teacher selection process is working well by tracking the teacher retention rate. Consider soliciting feedback from new teachers on the effectiveness of any mentoring or training program by giving them a simple pre- or post-survey.

2. **Identify student outcomes that need to be—and can realistically be—tracked.** It's important to think carefully about whether an outcome can truly be assessed. For example, an organization might like to know whether people who study yoga while incarcerated experience lower recidivism rates. Getting accurate data on this issue, however, would be impossible without investing in an extremely expensive, sophisticated study (and quite difficult even then).

   Often, program providers are legally prohibited from tracking people outside the context of their class. Even when this is not the case, tracking students post-release would be logistically impossible for providers. Further, defining recidivism can be tricky. Being arrested for a technical parole violation, for example, should not be equated with committing a serious crime.

Generally speaking, the easiest way to generate meaningful data on student experiences is by asking them to self-report. For example, simple five-point scales can be used to measure key outcomes such as levels of pain, stress, anxiety, and/or self-respect, along with incidences of insomnia, anger, conflict, and so on. Ideally, students should be provided with a range of ways to self-report that take different styles of personal expression and/or literacy levels into account (e.g., surveys, focus groups, artwork that addresses a question posed).

3. **Determine whether the facility or program site collects any relevant data.** Often, facilities conduct some form of data tracking on their own. If so, they may be willing to share these records. If possible, yoga service providers are encouraged to thoroughly discuss data collection and program evaluation plans with their point of contact before they are finalized to maximize any potential coordination and increase cooperation and buy-in.

4. **Find or develop simple data collection instruments.** Before investing time in creating data collection instruments, find out what others are doing. It's possible that a partner or host organization already has an evaluation process in place that can be joined, utilized independently, or adapted with minor modifications.

That said, it's not difficult to design simple data collection instruments. These could include pre- and post-student surveys, staff interview questions, teacher assessments, and open-ended feedback questions such as: "What did you find most helpful about this program? How do you think it could be improved"?

As much as possible, providers are advised to collect data using the same instruments so that it is consistent and can be compared over time. When designing or selecting data collection instruments, be sure to remain mindful of the language preferences, cultural sensitivities, literacy skills, and educational levels of those from whom information will be solicited.

5. **Obtain approval for any surveys to be given to students.** Yoga service providers should always follow facility protocols. Any program surveys must be preapproved. In addition to content, logistics such as clearance to bring papers and writing instruments into class on certain dates should be considered. Often, certain releases from the facility will need to be signed. When working with youth, parental notification is usually required. Yoga service providers should understand legal and administrative requirements, and meet them thoroughly. Be aware that it may be difficult to get approval for meaningful assessment instruments from facilities.

6. **Set up a timetable for data collection, analysis, and reporting.** Data collection needs to be done frequently enough to be meaningful but not so often as to be redundant, annoying, or obtrusive. A well-designed program evaluation will feel meaningful to those participating in it. People generally like having the opportunity to share their experiences, provide feedback, and voice their thoughts and opinions. Think into what sort of timetable is workable, useful, and respectful to the time constraints of those involved.

   Understand that collecting data is not the final step—the data need to be analyzed, considered, digested, and shared with stakeholders in an accessible and meaningful form. Then, there needs to be a process in which what's learned is leveraged to improve the program for staff, teachers, students, and program sites.

   Be realistic about the fact that this will take time. But remember that it is time well spent—and worth the investment. Having strong data collection and program evaluation protocols in place tremendously increases your chances of obtaining funding, attracting valuable allies, and growing your organization in healthy and empowering ways.

7. **Respect confidentiality.** It's imperative that yoga service providers be impeccable with their attention to releasing identifying information when reporting back to funders or their community. They might ask,

"Am I truly uplifting students with storytelling and the information being shared?" When in doubt, they should be conservative and put concern for the students first.

> "We partnered with a local university's justice studies department. The assistant professor sent interns into our sites to collect data objectively. The assistant professor was able to publish two articles and give her interns work, and we got our evaluation—a win-win all around."

Consider Partnerships. More well-established yoga service organizations might want to consider a partnership with a reputable local university or research institute to conduct program evaluation and related research. Often, student interns can collect data under the supervision of their professors. When such arrangements give them the opportunity to conduct original field research and data collection, and write reports and publish articles as a result, they can generate significant benefit for the academic researchers and yoga service provider alike.

If such an opportunity seems like it might be available, providers should consider the following before entering into an agreement:

- Make sure the facility/program site understands the proposed partnership and is okay with it.

- If working with students, ensure that they have faculty supervision—or, better yet, that a professor is heavily involved in the work.

- Make sure to introduce new research people appropriately. Set up orientations and trainings so that they understand the yoga program thoroughly, and so that they also know how to work respectfully and kindly with teachers, staff, students, correctional officers, and others whom they may encounter in the course of their work.

- Consider whether there might be conflicts between the needs of the academics/researchers involved and the needs of the program. If so, determine whether these are resolvable or whether the proposed partnership should be scratched.

- Do whatever can be done to avoid the possibility of students feeling exploited or being triggered. Any researchers involved with program work should share the program commitment to trauma-informed practices.

ORGANIZATIONAL DEVELOPMENT: BUILD A CONTINUUM OF CARE

Organizations should consider partnering with systems of reentry and continuation of care, where permitted.

The process of reentry, or transitioning from being incarcerated into everyday life, is tremendously under-resourced and unsupported in the United States. As much as possible, yoga service organizations should consider how they might continue to support formerly incarcerated students post-release. Such support could include continued access to yoga, ideally through dedicated, accessible classes. Additionally or alternatively, it might encompass making connections with or providing other services that support vital human needs such as employment, housing, and health care.

The extent to which engaging in such a "continuum of care" is feasible depends on organizational capacity and relevant laws in the program's jurisdiction. Many states prohibit organizations, professionals, and volunteers who have worked with incarcerated people "on the inside" from contacting them "on the outside." If this is the case in the program's area, yoga service providers might consider joining forces with other individuals and organizations working to provide needed services to system-involved people and change relevant policies to support the development of high-quality reentry programming.

> "A 'continuum of care' mindset is super important.
> We are always on the lookout for anywhere our
> youth aggregate 'on the outs' so that we can
> reconnect with them and help them continue their
> yoga practice. Community youth agencies have been
> very welcoming to these partnerships."

Learn the Local Landscape. Given that legal restrictions and reentry programming vary across jurisdictions, the first task is to find out what exists in the program's locale. Yoga service providers might ask contacts at the program site for information. They can inquire with other organizations providing relevant services in local communities. They might also see what exists online.

Whenever possible, yoga service providers should be present at stakeholder meetings within the facility and on the outside, so that they are in the loop about what other programs exist. This can help them decide what kind of aftercare they can offer and/or what is being provided by other organizations that they can connect their students with. This will allow teachers to better understand their role within the larger ecosystem and prevent them from overextending themselves. Being connected to other organizations is a great opportunity to build bridges for students when possible.

Build Bridges. Once program providers understand the relevant legal parameters and organizational landscape, they can turn to strengthening their contribution to a continuum of care. Of course, this will require substantial organizational capacity and won't be feasible for start-ups. Still, it is never too early to begin gathering information, making connections, and thinking into how the program might be able to contribute to post-release programs in the future.

If feasible, providers are encouraged to consider how best to create pathways for students to reengage with the organization post-release. They should be aware of any rules about being in contact with formerly incarcerated people.

The Department of Corrections has a process for this that must be followed. Providers should be willing to adapt the program as necessary to be effective on the outside without compromising quality or trauma-informed principles.

If the organization grows to the point where it is able to offer continuum of care services, providers can think into how best to get the word out to people who may be interested. Building formal and informal relationships with other relevant organizations in the program locale will likely be most useful. Additional options leaders can consider include requesting that the host site put information about the yoga program in whatever introduction and exit materials they distribute, and trying to connect with parole boards to let them know of any post-release services offered.

6

YOGA AS COMPLEMENTARY HEALTH CARE

The need for improved physical and mental health provision within the criminal justice system is great. This makes it particularly important to consider how yoga could be integrated into a broader array of system-based services as a complementary health care practice. This chapter provides an overview of key considerations for accomplishing this ambitious yet vitally important goal based on the experience of contributors whose organizations have navigated this process successfully.

Although achieving this level of health system integration is relatively rare and requires a high level of organizational development, it is something that individual teachers and yoga service organizations should understand and perhaps aspire to. Conversely, it's vital that health care professionals—as well as wardens, correctional officers, and others working in the criminal justice system—understand the possibilities of yoga in this regard. When offered by a team of well-trained instructors who understand how to work in partnership with other health care providers, yoga can make a signal contribution to system-provided health care.

The potential ripple effects of improved health outcomes for system-involved people are many, including better working conditions for system staff, better relationships between incarcerated people and their children and families, and better work and life prospects for them post-release. Given that yoga is comparatively an inexpensive addition to any set of health care services, it makes enormous sense to grow its status as a complementary health modality in the criminal justice system from both a humanistic and economic perspective.

COMPLEMENTARY HEALTH: UNDERSTAND THE FIELD

Individual teachers and yoga service organizations should invest in understanding and staying current on best practices and evidence-based methodologies in the health service field.

Many system-involved people have significant health issues. The vast majority are low-income and have historically lacked access to insurance.[14] Chronic disease is prevalent among the incarcerated, who suffer from comparatively higher rates of tuberculosis, HIV, hepatitis B and C, arthritis, diabetes, and STDs. More than half have mental health issues including but not limited to anxiety, depression, mania, and psychotic disorders. In local jails, this increases to 64 percent. The majority of incarcerated people with mental health issues also struggle with substance abuse and addiction.

Commonly, these issues are rooted in complex trauma. (See chapter 2, "Training and Staffing," for a discussion of trauma and trauma-informed yoga.) System-involved individuals with mental health issues are more likely to have been homeless and less likely to have been employed in the year prior to incarceration. They are more likely to report a history of physical and/or sexual abuse. Most are members of marginalized social groups who have collectively experienced trauma around discrimination, poverty, and dehumanization (Gates, 2014).

System-Based Services. Although correctional facilities are legally required to provide health care to incarcerated individuals, service provision varies significantly across states and among facilities. Many prisons hire independent doctors

---

14 Although the Affordable Care Act (ACA) expanded insurance access significantly, its implementation has varied tremendously among states. Further, at the time of this writing, the ACA is under strong attack from the Trump Administration, which hopes to "repeal and replace" it in ways that promise to restrict access to low-income people severely.

or contract with private or hospital staff to provide care. Some larger prisons have infirmaries on-site. Most piece together some sort of hybrid system.

In jails, health care is primarily provided through contracts with local health care providers such as public hospitals or other safety-net providers. Some large jails have on-site primary care, pharmacy, and mental health and substance abuse centers.

Examples of specific health services that should be (but are not necessarily) provided include but are not limited to:

- Pediatric, prenatal, oncological, geriatric, terminal illness, and hospice care

- Support for parents of young children (0 to 5 years) and teen parents, including early-prevention services

- Services for youth with special needs such as learning disabilities, autism spectrum, CSEC (commercial sexual exploitation of children), developmental delays, and mental and behavioral health

- Care for people with amputations, spinal cord injuries, traumatic brain injuries, and neurological conditions such as multiple sclerosis and Parkinson's disease

- Dedicated services for people housed in segregation units

Despite the legal mandate to provide health care, most incarcerated people go without it. One 2009 study found that among those with a persistent medical problem, approximately 14 percent of people in federal prisons, 20 percent of people in state prisons, and 68 percent of people in local jails did not receive a medical examination while incarcerated. About two-thirds of those in prisons and less than half in jails who had previously been taking psychiatric medication continued to do so after being incarcerated (Gates, 2014).

Cultural Competency. Yoga service providers seeking to integrate with existing health care providers should learn the basics coordinates of the fields they hope to coordinate with (e.g., mental health) if they are unfamiliar with it. Obviously, laypeople cannot become experts. They can, however, orient sufficiently to the field to make a real difference in terms of how well they'll be able to connect with professionals in it.

This involves developing a working knowledge of the most common health-related paradigms and philosophies of treatment, as well as the leading government, professional, and advocacy organizations in the field. Basic information on these matters should be easily accessible via Internet search. After that, yoga service providers can consider attending relevant professional meetings or possibly joining associations in their locales (e.g., a local chapter of National Alliance on Mental Illness, or NAMI).

"Speak the Language." Knowing how to "speak the language" of different professional and cultural groups is vital to effective communication. Yoga service providers should try to stay current with emerging language protocols in relevant health care fields. For example, the language of "trauma-informed care" has become well established not only in certain parts of the yoga world but in hospitals, schools, and prisons as well. Leveraging this shared language enables more effective, efficient, and collaborative communications between yoga service and system-based providers.

Another example of the importance of correct terminology would be knowing that the term "developmentally delayed" is acceptable, whereas "mentally retarded" is not. Even if well intentioned, using the wrong terms can erode trust and respect—and impede professional collaboration. The more that yoga service providers can stay attuned to how to speak effectively about issues of shared concern with health care providers and criminal justice staff, the better their chances of being well integrated into existing systems of care will be.

COMPLEMENTARY HEALTH: KNOW THE LOCAL HEALTH SERVICE COMMUNITY

Yoga service providers should educate themselves on the mission, scope of service, and activities of existing and potential health care community partners.

Once yoga service providers have a sense of the general field, they're ready to research the specifics of their local health care community. Program leaders should be on the lookout for potential organizational partners, individual supporters, and opportunities for learning and collaboration. This may include health care professionals, allied health providers, nonprofit organizations, and political, legal, and/or advocacy groups, among others.

Yoga service providers are encouraged to become informed on relevant programs, service providers, resources, contractors, grantees, facility staff, volunteers, educators, clergy, and others involved in local health care provisions, both wherever their programs are being offered and more generally. The best way to begin this learning process is to identify key individuals and organizations running similar programs in a given site (e.g., the same facility).

Are there any online or written materials that organizations are willing to share that discuss their history, philosophy, mission, vision, and/or methodology? Some organizations may also be willing to have in-person meetings to discuss their work and knowledge base more informally. Examples of personnel program leaders might want to contact include volunteer services coordinators, prison chaplains, and behavioral health services department members such as program coordinators or clinicians.

Coordinating Services. The more that yoga service providers develop an understanding of who's providing health care services in their program site and how they're doing it, the more yoga programs can be structured to complement those services. For example, a yoga service organization seeking to work with an addiction treatment program should first request information on its treatment methodology, treatment schedule, and average treatment timelines. Then, whatever yoga programming is proposed can be adapted as necessary to dovetail with existing structures and services.

COMPLEMENTARY HEALTH: CULTIVATE PARTNERS AND ALLIES

Yoga service providers should develop partnerships and alliances with local health care providers.

Once there's an understanding of the local health care landscape, yoga service providers are ready to start cultivating partners and allies. They can observe, attend, and, if appropriate, join other organizations. They should be respectful and discrete about participating in any sort of in-person encounter while in the information-gathering process, however. That said, program providers should feel comfortable requesting to attend events such as a nonprofit board meeting, health program treatment team meeting, or a "town hall" meeting for local agencies. In most cases, a key team member from the yoga program, such as the executive director or volunteer services coordinator, will be welcome to attend.

Yoga service providers should seek collaborators whose knowledge base and contributions promise to expand the program's capacity to deliver integrated, holistic, and sustainable services. Examples of potential partners include community-based dialectical behavioral therapy providers, nonviolent communication facilitators, and mental health providers trained in attachment theory and trauma-informed and gender-responsive methodologies.

Collaborative Evaluation. Yoga service providers seeking to demonstrate improved health outcomes should collaborate with partners to determine research protocols that evaluate reasonable and measurable outcomes. They can explore what it makes sense to evaluate together. Examples of possible measures include staff-reported changes in the frequency of behavioral issues and individual self-reports on the quantity of hours slept.

Program leaders need to be realistic about whether desired-outcomes measures are truly achievable. For example, it is more scientific to measure changes in stress levels by means of regular cortisol testing rather than self-reports. Implementing such a procedure, however, requires a level of financial, professional, and logistical resources that are only available to exceptionally well-funded research studies (which, unfortunately, rarely exist in the yoga service field).

Health service partners should have a shared interest in figuring out the best evaluation that can be done together. If partners are available and willing, yoga service providers are encouraged to work with them to create measurable outcomes that illustrate how their program contributes to the overall system of health care provision. Ideally, this will be of benefit for all involved, helping to improve services for students while documenting their value to existing and potential funders, partners, and others.

COMPLEMENTARY HEALTH:
KNOW SCOPE OF PRACTICE

Yoga service providers should have clarity regarding their scope of practice and how it interfaces with those of their partners.

To work as part of a complementary health team, it is vital that yoga service providers understand their own scope of practice and how it relates to those of their team partners. Some programs and facilities have well-structured health care teams; others do not. Well-established yoga service providers should seek to find out what teams, if any, exist at their site and join them if possible. Newer teachers and organizations should hold off on seeking to join professional teams until they feel confident of their capacity to take on another layer of coordination and responsibility.

Yoga service providers should be clear with themselves and others concerning the scope of what can and cannot be offered. The more that this division of labor is understood and appreciated by all concerned, the more well designed and coordinated health care services will be—and the more that students, clients, and patients will benefit.

Health care teams that yoga service providers may encounter and seek to integrate themselves into include:

- **Multidisciplinary Teams (MDTs).** As noted previously, MDTs do not exist at every facility. Where established, however, yoga teachers should seek to be invited and gain clearance to attend. When participating in an MDT, teachers might try to offer team members a training to acquaint them with core yoga tools taught (e.g., breathing and mindfulness techniques) in the program. By the same token, they can try to participate in relevant trainings offered by other team members or provided by an external agency to the MDT as a whole.

- **Specialty Mental Health Teams.** When working at sites that include specialty mental health teams, teachers should seek to adapt their yoga program to complement the existing protocols and methods of the other team as much as possible. For example, if the mental health team employs a treatment protocol that includes the use of "time-outs" to downregulate in the wake of a triggering incident, teachers should establish a space in their classes where students can move to a yoga mat to take their "time-out." Matching existing standards enables teachers to better manage the expectations of their students, communicate their respect for professional mental health providers, and help build a more effective and well-integrated system of mental health care provision.

- **Specialty Units.** Specialty health or housing units may include units for day treatment (e.g., adults in custody with developmental delays, traumatic brain injuries, or mental illnesses), rehabilitation services (individuals undergoing drug or alcohol detox and treatment), hospice units, segregation units, and so on. To work effectively and responsibly in such units, yoga service providers must understand the treatment services of the units, have appropriate specialized training (or a recognized equivalent), and collaborate with and defer to professional providers.

Appropriate specialized training may be health related and/or yoga specific. Examples of relevant health-related training might include brain development, mental illness, or the physiological and psychological processes of detoxification from drugs or alcohol. Yoga-specific training might include adaptive yoga (e.g., chair-based practice) or language choices (understanding left- versus right-brain communications).

To maximize knowledge and coordination, well-established yoga service providers may wish to consider stipulating that if they are to work in a specialty unit, they must first have access to the training manuals and understand the treatment methods used by other providers.

COMPLEMENTARY HEALTH: KNOW TRAUMA-INFORMED PRINCIPLES

Yoga service providers must understand how to apply trauma-informed principles to both yoga and their work as part of a health services team.

Yoga service providers who have succeeded in setting up a partnership with allied health providers must have mutually agreed-upon trauma-response and -prevention protocols. As discussed in previous chapters, training and proficiency in trauma-informed yoga is a prerequisite for teaching yoga in any sort of criminal justice setting. Once an organization has developed to the point where it's ready to join a health service team, it needs to ensure that its understanding of trauma extends beyond the boundaries of yoga to facilitate coordination among health care partners and allies.

Crisis Management. Agencies, institutions, and organizations may have existing policies and procedures for managing a crisis or event in which one or more students, residents, clients, or adults in custody get triggered or excessively agitated. Yoga providers should know what these procedures are and demonstrate collaboration by adhering to them. They should not try to handle such situations on their own.

Providers should be aware that in the course of offering yoga or other wellness programming, it's easy to develop a level of familiarity with students that can tempt them to make requests of teachers that, if implemented, would breech such protocols. For example, all adults in custody need to be accounted for at all times. However, one student might ask another to sign in him or her for class. If this occurs and is not immediately corrected, this seemingly simple act puts the teacher, the organization, and the students at risk of losing the privileges of providing or attending the class.

Medications. Individual teachers and yoga service organizations must refrain from discussing or providing advice on any sort of medication issues, including alternative health care options, with health care partners and/or students. Even if yoga teachers have relevant professional training, expertise, or certification, they should never make suggestions concerning medication to students before, during, or after a class.

Secondary Trauma. As discussed in chapter 2, "Training and Staffing," anyone working with yoga in the criminal justice system should have a solid understanding of secondary trauma, including its development, symptoms, treatment, and proactive strategies to prevent it. Yoga service providers should take care, however, to avoid using the term "secondary trauma" with partners unless it is an established part of their culture and communications. In some cases, suggesting that staff may experience secondary trauma in the course of their work may be alienating. When in doubt, stick with the language of "wellness," "shift-readiness," and/or "resilience," which will likely be more well received.

7

FACILITY-BASED YOGA TEACHER TRAININGS

Although yoga teacher training programs for incarcerated people are rare, several of the contributors to this book have developed and implemented them successfully. This chapter shares their experience, knowledge, and insights regarding how best to envision, structure, implement, navigate, and evaluate YTT programs for incarcerated people in correctional facilities. Establishing such a training is an ambitious endeavor that should only be considered by highly experienced teachers and well-established, high-capacity organizations. That said, it is possible and can be highly rewarding for all involved.

Because facility-based YTTs provide a means of training yoga teachers who are part of the community they wish to serve, they offer an incomparable means of rooting the practice of yoga more organically in communities where it would otherwise likely be absent or be offered by only teachers with profoundly different life experiences than those of their students. For these reasons and more, it is recommended that committed yoga service providers think seriously about the possibility of having a long-term goal of setting up a yoga teacher training program "on the inside" when they have the experience and capacity to do so.

FACILITY-BASED TRAININGS: GAIN DOC COOPERATION

Yoga service organizations should work closely with appropriate facility and DOC staff to determine whether a YTT program is possible.

Setting up a YTT in a correctional facility requires the consent and cooperation of top DOC administrators and staff. Beyond securing permission, the more buy-in there is from relevant DOC people, the more smoothly the program will run and the more successful it will be. Yoga service leaders who wish to pursue this work should therefore seek to develop and maintain the strongest partnership with facility administrators possible.

There is no single answer to the question of how best to start fostering such relationships, as it's dependent on what sorts of prior connections exist. If a yoga service organization has a strong preexisting relationship with its state DOC, it can begin discussions of what sort of program might work in one or more facilities at headquarters. If an organization has no such high-level connections to build on, it might start by developing promising relationships within a local facility or system office, and then work up to higher-level authorities from there.

In some localities, it may be possible to partner with a different social service organization (whether yoga related or not) that already has experience offering education and training programs on the inside. This is definitely worth investigating before setting out to develop a new program on one's own.

FACILITY-BASED TRAININGS:
SET PROGRAM PARAMETERS

Yoga service providers and DOC leaders should work together to establish basic program parameters such as location, timetable, and intended populations served.

Yoga service organizations will need to develop the basic parameters of their YTTs in consultation with DOC administrators. These include where the training would be held, who'd be eligible to participate in it, what study materials could be made available to students, and what the weekly schedule and overall timetable would be.

Location. The question of which facility might best house a training should be discussed in detail. For a YTT to run smoothly, facility staff must have the capacity—and the willingness—to provide the support needed to allow teachers to work with students for extended periods of time on a regular basis. This includes not only a substantial number of contact hours, in which the teacher trainers work directly with student trainees, but also enabling students to access independent-study materials such as books, articles, videos, and so on. Some YTT programs also supplement teacher-student contact hours with remote learning (e.g., weekly conference calls).

Schedule. Yoga service providers and DOC administrators must agree on what sort of schedule is workable. Alternative models include: (1) a 40-week (9- to 10-month) timetable with twice-weekly class meetings, or (2) one longer immersion session per month, supplemented by homework in between.

Students. The question of what sort of student to target is critical. For example: Should the program be in a men's or women's facility? Can students be released from work duties as needed to participate in the training? Should it be geared toward students who are slated for release in a few years or to people with life sentences? Who will the student trainees be prepared to teach if they successfully complete the program, and where? Program goals and curriculum structure should mesh with who is being served.

Facility Transfers. In some cases, the best students for a YTT program will not all be in the same facility. In such cases, it may be possible to transfer trainees to a different facility for the duration of the yoga teacher training program. Of course, this requires a high level of buy-in from the state DOC. At least two different state DOCs have, however, successfully transferred student trainees from geographically far-flung locales into one centrally located facility for the full duration of the YTT (and then back to their original facilities again when it was over). In both cases, the DOC's interest in the YTT program was that it offered a means of bringing yoga to remotely located facilities where it is difficult, if not impossible, to provide it otherwise.

Yoga service providers should be aware that students may not want to go back to these remote locales once they have the opportunity to be housed in a more central location. If this is the agreement, however, they will have no choice but to comply. In such circumstances, care should be taken to prepare emotionally, psychologically, and spirituality for what is almost guaranteed to be a challenging YTT graduation experience.

FACILITY-BASED TRAININGS: DEVELOP CURRICULUM AND STUDY MATERIALS

YTT providers should develop their curriculum and study materials based on best existing models and the particularities of their program.

Offering YTTs in correctional facilities is a complex endeavor. It is important to learn from the best models available in the field before attempting to develop a new program. That said, each facility-based YTT will inevitably have its own particular set of opportunities, challenges, commitments, and constraints. Seeking a judicious mixture of the best existing models and the specificities of emerging ones is the most promising means of developing a curriculum.

Study Materials and Resources. YTT programs must navigate the same issues of having yoga mats and props available for student use as other facility-based classes. Beyond standard practice materials, YTTs must develop and arrange student access to program supports such as videos, books, and recorded lectures. Students may need special permission to have items such as pen and paper in order to complete written homework assignments. Ideally, in-person meetings can be supplemented by remote learning arrangements via video- or teleconferencing with teacher trainers.

Different facilities will have different rules governing what YTT programs can and cannot provide students. Yoga service organizations are encouraged to make every attempt to anticipate relevant logistics and address challenges proactively. For example, if a facility only allows incarcerated people to have three books in their cells at a time, YTT staff should attempt to stock ample numbers of required texts in the prison library and ensure that these readings will be as accessible to students as possible.

YA Registration. YTT programs should consider whether to pursue Yoga Alliance (YA) accreditation carefully. Where YA registration is being sought, the yoga service organization will need to become a YA Registered Yoga School (RYS). What makes sense will depend on the particularities such as where the program is located and who it is designed to serve.

In some states, yoga teachers who lack YA registration cannot offer classes in studios, gyms, and other public settings. In others, registration is not required and may not even be on potential employers' radar screens. Thus, depending on where a program is located and whether the students it serves are slated for release in the near future or not, YA registration may or may not be important.

YTT providers may also wish to consider whether YA registration might feel significant to students on a more personal level. Some students may value the sense of accomplishment gained from meeting YA criteria highly. One YTT provider reports that this tends to be true with students even when they are incarcerated and as of yet have no practical need for the credential. That said, whatever psychological and emotional benefits the YA credential may confer must be balanced with the more concretely pragmatic needs of the students, facility, and provider.

Should YTT providers choose to pursue YA certification for participants, they will need to consider how to maintain YA certification standards and continuing education requirements. If YTT providers have the capacity and intend to provide such components on a long-term basis, they're advised to include this in their preliminary training proposal and budget. They might consider the length of the relationship with those they are training. Will this mentorship and support continue upon reentering the community or be maintained throughout long-term and life sentences? YTT providers should be clear about their capacity and commitment with both the facility and participants.

FACILITY-BASED TRAININGS:
SET REALISTIC GOALS

YTTs should set realistic goals for students, the facility, and the yoga service organization of which they're a part.

It's crucial that YTT programs have a clearly defined set of overarching goals that pull together the specifics of the curriculum. What goals are appropriate will vary depending on the types of students being served and how the training fits into the larger organizational contexts of both the yoga service provider and the correctional system.

Yoga service providers should be careful to set realistic goals. For example, it may seem attractive to frame a yoga teacher training as a post-release employment resource if it's designed for students who are slated for release reasonably soon after it ends. Given the difficult job market facing yoga teachers, however, this may not be a realistic goal. This is particularly true if it's implied or assumed that teaching yoga is likely to be sufficient as a sole source of income. Regardless of whether they've been system-involved or not, most people find it difficult to make a living as a yoga teacher today. It is more realistic to assume that it could provide supplemental income, build a post-release employment history, and be a source of social connection and personal accomplishment.

As noted above, different facilities will have different goals of their own when it comes to allowing YTT programs inside. For example, there may be a goal of training yoga teachers who can offer classes in remote facilities where no other programs (perhaps of any sort) are present. YTT program developers should have a clear understanding of the motivations and goals of the facility and DOC of which they are part, and feel confident that those missions are in alignment with their own intentions and integrity. If this is not the case, the program should not start until these differences have been resolved.

Yoga service providers are advised to reflect carefully on what their internal organizational goals are with regard to launching a facility-based yoga teacher training. Given the huge investment of time and resources it will involve, there should be a clear understanding of their personal and organizational motivations and commitments. Coming to clarity on this is critical and should involve in-depth research, reflection, and discussion before any decision is made.

FACILITY-BASED TRAININGS:
DEVELOP BUDGET AND SEEK FUNDING

YTT programs should develop detailed budgets and fundraise as needed to meet costs.

There are significant costs associated with running a facility-based YTT. These may include teacher time (although some programs use volunteers), administrative hours, in-house training materials (manuals, videos, etc.), travel reimbursement (for teachers with substantial commutes), required readings (books, articles, etc.), and yoga mats and props.

The sum total of such costs is likely to be quite high for a yoga service organization, which is typically a very small organization run on a shoestring (or zero) budget. One well-established organization estimated that it cost approximately $50,000 to run its facility-based YTT. This sum included paying teachers for prep and teaching time; travel (based on mileage reimbursement); administrative time; materials and yoga props; and post-release mentoring and support for program grads.

In some cases, the entire YTT budget must be fundraised privately, such as when no public funds are available. In other states, some public funding may be available. It is highly unlikely, however, that state monies will ever cover the primary, let alone full, costs. Consequently, any yoga service organization that hopes to run a facility-based YTT must first develop substantial fundraising capacities.

"Some of our graduates have started to teach yoga classes, which is of course very exciting. However, coordinating their classes with individual facilities has been challenging at best. It is wise to consider how long you plan to work with graduates of your program. In our case, many of our graduates are in for life. Supporting their ongoing study and learning limits our ability to offer more YTTs unless we significantly expand our staff capacity."

FACILITY-BASED TRAININGS: SELECT STUDENTS CAREFULLY

YTT programs should have a well-constructed application process that enables them to assess and select student trainees carefully.

Facility-based YTT programs will be investing a huge amount of time and energy into a small group of student trainees. There may be substantially more people who want to do the training than there are slots available. It's very important to select students carefully. Having people in the program who are a poor fit for it will drag everyone down and make what is already a challenging endeavor substantially more so.

YTT programs should work as closely with DOC staff as possible to develop an appropriate and well-constructed application process. Different methods used by established programs for selecting students include:

- Prospective students are asked to fill out an application and submit three letters of recommendation from specific types of people (e.g., a counselor or probation officer). YTT staff review these materials in conjunction with the prison chaplain.

- Prospective students must obtain a recommendation from their case manager. Then they are eligible to submit an application.

- Prospective students must complete a six-month prerequisite program, attending a minimum of one (out of a total of three available) yoga class per week. They must also attend a bimonthly discussion group and at least one meditation class monthly (out of a total of one offered weekly).

While such requirements may seem onerous, it is important to realize that running a YTT in a facility will require an enormous investment on the part of both the yoga service provider and facility staff. Admitting students into the program who are a bad fit for it may jeopardize the quality of the program and perhaps even its continued viability.

FACILITY-BASED TRAININGS: UTILIZE MATURE, HIGHLY QUALIFIED TEACHERS

Teachers leading YTT programs must have exceptionally high levels of training, maturity, and experience.

As discussed in chapter 2, "Training and Staffing," yoga teachers who work in the criminal justice system should have a higher minimum level of training than those who work in studios and gyms. By extension, the qualifications of those who lead facility-based YTTs must be even higher. Yoga teacher training is an intensive process that places significant demands on students under any circumstances. Leading a YTT in a correctional setting is substantially more challenging. As such, it requires teachers with an exceptionally high degree of training, maturity, and experience.

If suitable teachers are not available, a proposed program should not move forward. Otherwise, it runs substantial risk of doing more harm than good.

YTT Demands. The typical YTT includes a minimum of 180 hours of in-person instruction. (As discussed in chapter 2, "Training and Staffing," the 200-hour standard is set by Yoga Alliance and widely followed in the field. YA requires at least 180 "contact hours" within this 200-hour framework.) This means that teachers will be working very closely with students for many hours during a substantial period of time. These students are likely to have personal histories of trauma. They are also coping with the inherently traumatic experience of incarceration while living in an environment where acute traumatic events may be seen or experienced unpredictably and frequently.

As discussed in chapter 4, "Relationship Building," yoga teachers should always maintain appropriate personal and professional boundaries. They are not working with students to become their friends. They are not therapists. (Even if trained as therapists, while working as a yoga teacher that is not their role.) Yet, they are attempting to offer an intensive, multidimensional training that prioritizes experiential knowledge.

Most yoga teacher trainings include not only how to instruct *asana* (that is, the poses performed in a typical yoga class) but material on yoga philosophy, anatomy and physiology, personal reflection, group discussion, spiritual exploration, and more. Balancing the commitment to offer an in-depth training, connect with students individually and collectively, and maintain appropriate boundaries is complex, challenging work.

Selection Criteria. All teachers being considered to lead a facility-based YTT should meet the requirements for teaching yoga in the criminal justice system specified in chapter 2, "Training and Staffing." Beyond this, it is worth considering:

- **Track Record.** Has the potential teacher trainer served with the organization providing the YTT for a significant period of time? People who are known to work well with the organization will most likely continue to do so.

- **In-House Training.** If the yoga service organization offering the YTT provides a training for its own teachers, did the applicant take it? If not, she or he should.

- **Relevant Training and Experience.** Yoga teachers with professional training and experience in fields such as social work bring important background to their YTT work, even if not acting in that professional capacity while teaching yoga.

- **Life Experience.** Teachers who embody maturity based on life experience and personal development bring critical qualities to a YTT that formal credentials cannot. In many cases, an appropriate level of personal maturity will correlate with a more advanced age (e.g., over 40). In other cases, it will not.

- **Diversity.** YTTs should strive to recruit a group of teachers who embody a diversity of body types, racial/ethnic identities, and genders. It is critical to demonstrate to students that not only one type of person is qualified to teach yoga. Living examples of this fact are needed to back up words to the same effect.

FACILITY-BASED TRAININGS: TEACH IN TEAMS

Every YTT session should have a team of at least two teachers leading it.

It's preferable to have at least two teachers present and working together as a team for any YTT session. Ideally, this should be the case for regular (non-YTT) yoga classes as well. Because of the higher demands placed on students in a teacher training context, however, it is even more important in this context.

Precisely how the team works will vary both among programs and within any given program's classes. One common arrangement is to have one teacher lead the session while the other observes how the class is responding and/or role models how students might engage with the material. Here, it's often useful to switch the roles of lead and support facilitator within the course of the same session. This demonstrates that different people can play leadership roles and that leaders can also shift positions to follow and cooperate with others.

Some YTT programs utilize a third teacher who observes the session and gives feedback to the two lead teachers after class. Either way, it is a best practice to have more than one teacher so that another can observe students more carefully while also role modeling and co-facilitating. Having more people also provides backup in case of unexpected difficulties, which are likely to occur given the unpredictable and highly challenging nature of the environment.

FACILITY-BASED TRAININGS:
SUPPORT STUDENT SAFETY AND WELL-BEING

YTTs should support student safety and well-being in the program and surrounding environment.

To be effective, yoga teacher trainings need to create a sense of safety and trust among students, both individually and collectively. Without it, trainees cannot engage in the personal reflection, self-exploration, and sharing necessary to make the experience meaningful. YTT program leaders should be acutely aware, however, that creating a safe container for yoga training within the context of a correctional facility necessarily exposes students to a distinctive set of challenges and risks. Programs must be designed and teachers prepared to mitigate these risks proactively, so that the greatest conditions of safety can be realized for students both within YTT sessions and beyond them.

Institutional Hazards. Even in the best of circumstances, serious yoga students often find it challenging to transition from the intimacy and intensity of an in-depth class back into "regular life." The stress of such transitions is magnified beyond measure when experienced in the context of a correctional facility, where students have no control over the basic parameters of daily life and may be routinely and unpredictably exposed to emotionally wrenching and even physically dangerous events.

For example: If a YTT is held in a maximum-security prison, students may be required to be strip searched every time that they participate in a training session. In lower-security settings, students may be required to be strip searched on particular occasions (e.g., visitation days, when family members get to visit their loved ones), which may coincide with YTT sessions. Transitioning from a yoga training that is designed to be a heart-opening, soul-searching experience into such a dehumanizing and invasive one is likely to be challenging and potentially traumatic.

YTT staff must also recognize that incarcerated people may pose dangers to one another. Not all of the challenges or risks come from the institution. They also come from students' peers. The human dynamics created in a correctional facility logically trend toward defensiveness and mistrust. Personal information tends to be carefully guarded, as some can use it against others in dangerously aggressive and manipulative ways. Yet, a YTT setting is designed to facilitate openness and trust. Negotiating these opposing dynamics in ways that maximize student safety requires tremendous skill and knowledge on the part of YTT leaders and teachers.

Gender Dynamics. YTT curriculum and instruction should be gender sensitive. Reports from experienced yoga teacher trainers in the field indicate that the interpersonal dynamics among students tend to vary consistently between genders. Although individuals and groups will of course vary, the general pattern observed is that women tend to form quasi-familial structures that create a relatively high degree of interpersonal emotional intensity. In contrast, men tend to start out as individuals who feel wary of one another but develop a sense of being a cohesive "band of brothers" over time. As a general rule, this means that the social dynamics among men may be easier for teacher trainers to work with. That said, YTT leaders should be scrupulous about avoiding projecting gender-based expectations onto students.

FACILITY-BASED TRAININGS:
MENTOR STUDENTS AND TEACHERS

YTTs should establish mentoring relationships for students and teachers alike.

Yoga teacher training programs "on the outside" generally provide group instruction with no individualized, one-on-one mentoring. This common arrangement is not appropriate in a criminal justice context, given its inescapable intensity, challenge, and risk. Ideally, students and teachers alike should have ongoing, individualized support from knowledgeable, experienced mentors. While mentoring can be set up in different ways, whatever arrangement is chosen should provide individualized support as consistently and effectively as is reasonably possible.

One experienced provider set up a system that matched each of the 12 students in the program with 12 different yoga teacher mentors. These teacher mentors, in turn, received ongoing mentorship themselves from the executive director of the organization, who has decades of relevant experience. Once student trainees were able to lead their own classes, mentors would attend to observe and give feedback. In this way, students are not simply trained to teach but also mentored through the process of beginning to teach classes themselves. At the same time, the next layer of mentoring between teacher trainers and the lead teacher is ongoing.

This level of individualized support is not always possible, however. Some facilities prohibit one-on-one meetings between teachers and students. Some YTT programs don't have the capacity to assign mentors to each student individually. In such cases, a good option is to set up regular mentoring sessions co-facilitated by two teacher trainers. One teacher can lead a group activity, while the other remains available for individual questions and concerns. This arrangement allows for both efficiencies in time and staff while also creating a time and place for individual questions, feedback, and discussion.

FACILITY-BASED TRAININGS: EXPECT UNEXPECTED CHALLENGES

YTT leaders, teachers, and staff should expect to encounter unexpected challenges and be prepared to troubleshoot as needed.

Even the most well-planned and well-implemented YTT will likely encounter completely unanticipated challenges. Being psychologically and emotionally prepared to grapple with unexpected issues and problems will help the program succeed and minimize whatever spin-off issues or secondary problems might otherwise arise.

Some of what experienced providers have encountered along these lines in the past include the following:

- One of the work units that some YTT students were assigned to was put under investigation. Consequently, the entire unit went on lockdown for the weekend, causing the students to miss that month's session.

- Individual YTT students were sent to solitary confinement and missed class as a result.

- A facility agreed to host a YTT on the condition that it include two "problem cases." These students did not have to meet the same admissions requirements as the rest of the class. Although ostensibly an effort to help these individuals, both were disruptive and difficult, and they eventually stopped showing up at all.

- One facility was exceptionally disorganized. Every week, it proved difficult, if not impossible, for staff to get the eight trainees into the right room on time. Sometimes, non-students would be brought to class instead. Other times, only half the names on the list of permitted students would be correct. Sometimes, yoga teachers would not be let in the building. Other times, their paperwork would mysteriously disappear.

- One facility was set up so that yoga teachers had to leave the building in order to use the restroom. Once they left, they would not be allowed back in for the entire day. No one flagged this issue to the YTT program before it started.

- One facility did not inform the lead teacher that she needed to order food trays for students in order for them to be able to eat during a daylong training. Without this information, no food was ordered or provided. The students had to go hungry all day.

- One facility has a rule stating that if the officer assigned to oversee the program is out sick or otherwise unavailable, the session must be canceled.

Solutions to such problems will vary depending on circumstances. However, some cushions can be proactively built into the YTT program. For example, it makes sense to put some extra training hours in the schedule beyond what's actually expected so that if sessions have to be canceled unexpectedly, it's easy to make up the lost hours.

Having clear guidelines for how student absences will be handled is also helpful. For example, one YTT had a rule that if students did something independently that caused them to be sent to solitary and miss a class, they'd have to make up the material on their own. However, if students missed class due to circumstances beyond their control, the YTT program would set up new sessions as needed to cover the missed material.

FACILITY-BASED TRAININGS:
HOLD A GRADUATION CEREMONY

If possible, YTTs should hold graduation ceremonies for students who complete the program.

Whether offered "inside" or "outside," high-quality yoga teacher training programs are intended to be deeply meaningful, even life-changing events. Completing one requires a substantial commitment on the part of the student. As such, it is appropriate to hold a graduation ceremony to celebrate and honor their success in finishing the program.

Each of the several contributors to this volume who arranged and/or participated in YTT graduation ceremonies in facilities agreed that the experience was deeply meaningful and important. Depending on what the facility allowed, attendees included students, their close friends, family members, other (non-YTT) yoga students at the facility, previous YTT graduates, YTT teachers and staff, yoga service provider board members and staff, correctional officers, and other criminal justice professionals.

Elements of graduation ceremonies have included conferring yoga teacher certificates to students, having selected students give speeches, bringing in outside food (fresh veggies and fruit, cheese and crackers, cake), holding a *kirtan* (music featuring call-and-response-style singing that's popular among many yoga practitioners), and having a yoga teacher who learned the practice while incarcerated and is now released and working as a yoga teacher speak about her experience.

Cautions. YTT program leaders should be very careful about how the issue of holding a graduation ceremony is broached with facility staff and criminal justice professionals initially. Until a program is well established enough to be broadly accepted, trusted, and valued, it is probably best to hold off on making this request.

Without laying the proper groundwork, it is possible that the idea of a celebratory ceremony could be seen as inappropriate or even offensive. YTT programs should be aware that such events definitely require additional work on the part of facility staff, who may need to obtain security clearances for outside guests, provide additional supervision for a gathering, and so on. Given such inevitable demands and potential sensitivities, it's best to move cautiously, establishing supportive relationships and a strong track record before seeking clearance.

Even when approval is obtained, planning and executing a successful gradu-ation ceremony requires substantial work. This is true in any context. Again, however, doing this within a facility is inevitably more difficult. While the effort is well worth it, it is a project that should not be undertaken without a realistic consideration of the likely challenges involved.

FACILITY-BASED TRAININGS: CONSIDER TEACHING OPPORTUNITIES CAREFULLY

YTTs should consider how to structure and/or facilitate teaching opportunities for their graduates carefully.

Generally speaking, yoga teacher training programs are valuable experiences whether graduates go on to teach yoga or not. In society at large, countless numbers of yoga enthusiasts have taken YTTs with no intention of ever teaching, simply for the opportunities for learning, growth, and personal development that they provide. That said, a good YTT program confers a valuable skill set that many graduates are deeply motivated to share with others (sometimes to their surprise, if this was not their original intent).

Facility-based YTTs should be expected to be similar to others in this regard. It should not be considered necessary to have graduates of a program teach yoga in order for it to be considered a valuable experience and worthwhile investment. (Outcomes can and should be measured in multiple ways; see chapter 5, "Orga-nizational Development.") That said, it is ideal for successful graduates to have opportunities to teach if they want to, whether while incarcerated or post-release.

Teaching in Facilities. Where possible, YTT leaders are encouraged to work proactively with DOC staff to create yoga teaching positions for graduates who will remain incarcerated for any substantial period post-training. Some state DOCs are eager to facilitate such arrangements; others will not consider it at all.

To some extent, what attitude prevails will depend on the personal relationships established between yoga service providers and the DOC in the past. In some cases, however, laws will govern what's allowed. This can vary enormously: One state may not allow incarcerated people to teach except as an assistant to an outside teacher. Another may allow them to lead classes independently and even pay a very minimal wage for it (e.g., $2.50 per class).

When considering how best to set up such classes, it is vital that all parties carefully consider how potential positions might play into preexisting power dynamics. Social relations in facilities tend to have very strong formal and informal hierarchies. By its very nature, the role of a teacher confers some degree of power. Setting up a new teaching position is likely to shift to some degree whatever social hierarchies exist. This can be problematic and even dangerous if not considered and handled carefully.

YTT leaders and DOC staff should work together to create positions that enable new teachers to be of service in safe and mutually beneficial ways. One strategy to consider is utilizing a team teaching model whenever possible. This attenuates power issues and provides more support to teachers and students alike.

Another model that has worked well is having YTT graduates only teach classes for people living on special units (i.e., dedicated quarters for incarcerated people dealing with addiction, traumatic brain injuries, mental illness, etc.). This arrangement provides extra support to people who really need it, generates buy-in from staff, and attenuates any sense of special privileges being conferred on new teachers among the general population. Of course, to work properly it may require additional training to address the specific needs of these students.

Teaching Post-Release. Again, the extent to which YTT programs can facilitate teaching opportunities for graduates will vary from state to state. In this case, the key question is whether state laws allow organizations to follow up with people they've worked with while incarcerated. If possible, YTT leaders should work with DOC staff to establish means of connecting with former students post-release. Beyond facilitating teaching opportunities, yoga service organizations should, if possible, connect them to a wider network of reentry supports. One strategy that yoga service providers may consider, where possible, is developing partnerships with yoga studios and/or community organizations interested in employing or otherwise supporting YTT grads.

Whenever employment options are considered, it is crucial to be honest about the fact that making a living as a yoga instructor is challenging under any circumstances. This should be made clear to participants and facility staff prior to commencing a YTT.

That said, teaching yoga can offer a meaningful employment experience that helps connect people to a supportive community and the wider society post-release. Further, as any good yoga instructor knows, teaching offers an excellent means of deepening one's own personal practice while helping others. The resultant synergy of personal growth and social service can be profoundly beneficial for all concerned.

CONCLUSION

AN EMERGING FIELD OF SERVICE

Prior to 2000, very few yoga classes were taught in a criminal justice setting, and what was provided typically focused heavily on traditional yoga philosophy. But during the past decade, more and more organizations dedicated to offering a more secular, psychophysiological, therapeutic approach to yoga have emerged. In the United States, this has resulted in a significant upswing in the number of jails and prisons offering yoga programs (Horton et al., 2016). At the same time, yoga is becoming more widely recognized and accepted as a valuable complementary therapy for trauma, recovery from addiction, and other issues that heavily impact criminal justice processes and outcomes.

Today, an estimated 250 to 300 jails, prisons, and court-ordered rehabilitation programs have yoga classes taught by outside program providers (i.e., individual yoga teachers and/or yoga service organizations). Most are state and county facilities located on the East or West Coasts; a few are federal institutions. An additional 50 to 75 offer classes taught by people who are currently incarcerated themselves. The number of facilities that allow such classes, as well as the number of incarcerated people who are ready to teach them, is growing rapidly.[15] The extent to which yoga is being offered in other parts of the criminal justice system (court-ordered programs, residential treatment centers, etc.) is unknown.

This growth in therapeutic yoga offerings in the criminal justice system provides a solid foundation on which to build. The purpose of this book

---

15 Personal communication with James Fox, founder and director of the Prison Yoga Project, July 2017.

is to provide an easily accessible means of learning from the collective experience, knowledge, and insight of leaders in this emerging field, so that further expansion can be done with as much quality and integrity as possible. While yoga can be an invaluable resource for people involved with or working in the criminal justice system, it must be appropriately adapted to meet their needs, concerns, and values if it is to be safe, therapeutic, and effective.

Some popular ways of teaching yoga are inappropriate for a criminal justice context and could even cause harm. Just because a practice is labeled "yoga" doesn't mean that it can't cause injury, trigger trauma, or simply alienate people who might enjoy it if it were adapted to meet their individual and environmental needs. Teaching yoga in ways that are appropriately trauma-informed, age appropriate, gender responsive, culturally competent, and aligned with relevant criminal justice rules, regulations, and procedures requires a significantly higher level of training, experience, and maturity than is necessary for an average studio- or gym-based class. Challenging in any context, teaching a high-quality yoga class is significantly more so in the exceptionally stressful and unpredictable context of the criminal justice system.

Yet teaching yoga in the criminal justice system is a challenge that the contributors to this book, as well as countless additional yoga service providers out in the field, have found profoundly rewarding and well worth the effort involved. Their shared passion and concern for this work is palpable and inspiring. That said, teaching in the criminal justice system is certainly not appropriate for all yoga teachers. Nor should it be. There are as many ways to be of service as there are individual teachers—and students. (And every good teacher knows that they remain perpetually a student.) Yoga teachers and others who believe in this work but don't feel called to engage in it directly can provide invaluable support in other ways that are needed and welcome.

As with any yoga instruction, what matters most is serving students by sharing the practice with them in ways that are safe, effective, accessible, and engaging. The fruits of this work in a criminal justice context are often beautifully inspiring.

They also provide a relatively low-cost means of leveraging results that more established (and likely more costly) interventions strive but fail to achieve.

In her study of formerly incarcerated men who had participated in a prison yoga program, Viorst (2017) found that the overwhelming majority described it as "more impactful than other prison programs on aggression, including San Quentin's 'Victim-Offender Education' (VOE) program, and 'Guiding Rage into Power' (GRIP), a program specifically built to prevent aggression" (p. 21). One approximately 55-year-old man who had been released from prison for three years and studied yoga while incarcerated for 10 explained the difference as follows:

> I've been to a lot of anger management things, and it's just talk. You can know that you're clenching up or clenching your fists, but unless you have a physical tool to slow things down . . . and those classes will teach breathing, but unless you've done the reps of inhaling and exhaling fully while doing asanas [yoga poses] . . . it's not something that I think comes easily to most people if it's not something you practice while doing something difficult. Like if you could move with your breath and not lose your breath under the stress of the movement or getting fatigued, then if you're getting hit with that kind of stressful situation and you can remember the breath, you've practiced it so much that it's easier to do. (Viorst, 2017, p. 21)

A recent first-of-its-kind report on the value of therapeutic somatic practices for system-involved girls published by Georgetown Law's Center on Poverty and Inequality supports these experiential findings. (While framed more broadly, the focus of this study was on trauma-informed yoga programs working with girls in youth detention centers.) Authors Epstein and González (2017) report that "unlike many interventions, the implementation of trauma-informed somatic programs is surprisingly cost-effective and highly sustainable" (p. 27). Demonstrated positive effects of participation in the trauma-informed yoga programs studied include: (1) improved self-regulation and other emotional development, (2) improved neurological and physical health, and (3) healthier relationships and parenting practices.

Given the low cost and high efficacy of TIY programs in the youth justice system, these researchers advocate increased public and private funding to support the expansion of high-quality, sustainable programming:

> We recommend consideration of state and county government support for these programs, as well as funding from private foundations. San Francisco County's juvenile hall yoga program and programs in San Mateo County, for example, operate under a block grant funded by California Board of State and Community Corrections; the Greater Cedar Rapids Community Foundation recently funded expansion of the yoga program in Linn County Juvenile Detention Center. Funding and infrastructure development can also be designed as public-private partnerships, because trauma-informed yoga programs for system-involved girls could be eligible for funding from private foundations that maintain health and wellness portfolios. Given the benefits of somatic interventions, resources from federal, state, and local governments aimed at improving physical, mental, and behavioral health outcomes are also viable funding streams. (Epstein & González, 2017, p. 27)

In sum, integrating high-quality yoga programs into the criminal justice system is a low-cost, high-value project that merits both public and private support.

Yoga alone cannot address the deep dysfunctions of the U.S. criminal justice system or transform the life circumstances of system-involved people. It can, however, play a critical role in supporting the physical and mental health—as well as the self-awareness, self-regulation, and positive empowerment—of those who practice it regularly. Such positive impacts on people who are involved with or work in the criminal justice system has ripple effects. It creates new openings for creative synergies with other therapeutic interventions, organizational improvements, and system-level reforms. The emerging field of yoga service in the criminal justice system has demonstrated its capacity to change countless lives for the better. Today, our task is to maximize its potential in ways that support a more healing, humane, and just system, society, and world for all.

APPENDIX A: Recommended Resources

The following books, films, and websites are recommended as additional resources for readers seeking to learn more about the U.S. criminal justice system and issues of mass incarceration, the psychology of trauma and trauma-informed yoga, and living and practicing yoga while incarcerated. Please note that these works do not duplicate those listed as References; they are being shared here as general resources and were not necessarily cited in the text.

U.S. CRIMINAL JUSTICE SYSTEM AND MASS INCARCERATION

Books

All Alone in the World: Children of the Incarcerated, Nell Bernstein (2007)

Breaking Women: Gender, Race, and the New Politics of Imprisonment, Jill A. McCorkel (2013)

Burning Down the House: The End of Juvenile Prison, Nell Bernstein (2016)

Invisible Punishment: The Collateral Consequences of Mass Imprisonment, Meda Chesney-Lind & Marc Mauer (2002)

The New Jim Crow: Mass Incarceration in the Age of Colorblindness, Michelle Alexander (2012)

On the Run: Fugitive Life in an American City, Alice Goffman (2015)

Race to Incarcerate, Marc Mauer & The Sentencing Project (2006)

Women Behind Bars: The Crisis of Women in the U.S. Prison System, Silja Talvi (2007)

Films

13th, directed by Ava DuVernay, Kandoo Films (2016)

Websites

The American Civil Liberties Union https://www.aclu.org

Bureau of Justice Statistics https://www.bjs.gov

The Sentencing Project http://www.sentencingproject.org

The Southern Poverty Law Center https://www.splcenter.org

PSYCHOLOGY OF TRAUMA

Books

The Body Keeps the Score: Brian, Mind, and Body in the Healing of Trauma, Bessel van der Kolk, MD (2015)

The Body Remembers: The Psychophysiology of Trauma and Trauma Treatment, Babbette Rothschild (2000)

Trauma Stewardship: An Everyday Guide to Caring for Self While Caring for Others, Laura van Dernoot Lipsky & Connie Burk (2009)

Waking the Tiger: Healing Trauma, Peter A. Levine (1997)

When the Body Says No: Understanding the Stress-Disease Connection, Gabor Maté, MD (2011)

TRAUMA-INFORMED YOGA

Books

Mindfulness and Yoga Skills for Children and Adolescents: 115 Activities for Trauma, Self-Regulation, Special Needs & Anxiety, Barbara Neiman (2015)

Overcoming Trauma Through Yoga: Reclaiming Your Body, David Emerson & Elizabeth Hopper, MD (2011)

Teaching Transformative Life Skills to Students: A Comprehensive Dynamic Mindfulness Curriculum, Bidyut Bose (2016)

Trauma-Sensitive Yoga in Therapy: Bringing the Body into Treatment, David Emerson (2015)

Yoga for Emotional Balance: Simple Practices to Help Relieve Anxiety and Depression, Bo Lozoff (2011)

Yoga for Emotional Trauma: Meditations and Practices for Healing Pain and Suffering, Mary NurrieStearns & Rick NurrieStearns (2013)

Yoga Nidra: A Meditative Practice for Deep Relaxation and Healing, Richard Miller (2010)

LIVING BEHIND BARS

Books

Be Free Where You Are, Thich Nhat Hanh (2002)

Dharma in Hell: the Prison Writings of Fleet Maull, Fleet Maull (2005)

Houses of Healing: A Prisoner's Guide to Inner Power and Freedom, Robin Casarjian (1995)

Letters from the Dhamma Brother: Meditation Behind Bars, Jenny Phillip (2008)

A Path for Healing and Recovery: Prison Yoga Project, James Fox (2011)

We are All Doing Time: A Guide to Getting Free, Bo Lozoff (1998)

A Woman's Practice: Healing from the Heart, Kath Meadows (2014)

APPENDIX B: Yoga Service Organizational Development Typology

Stage of Organizational Development	Staff Size and Compensation	Staff Roles
Start-up	Single individual or small group. Usually one determined leader. All volunteer.	Everyone does everything: admin, teaching, etc. Individual roles and how to coordinate them are often unclear.
Emerging	Single individual or small group (e.g., 1 to 5). All volunteer but perhaps with some "perks" (transportation reimbursement, etc.).	Clearer differentiation of leadership structure and staff roles, though still informal. Core group of teachers and others who cycle in and out.
Established	Small- to mid-size group (e.g., 5 to 15). Minimal compensation for core staff (usually one person) and teachers.	Well-established leadership position. Some regular administrative support. Stable set of qualified teachers. Dedicated grant writer (if nonprofit).
Mature	Mid-size to large group (e.g., 10 to 30). Executive director, staff, and yoga teachers compensated.	Formal executive director role and clearly defined staff positions. Stable set of well-qualified teachers. Established development director (if nonprofit).

Teacher Requirements, Training, and Mentoring	Organizational Form	Fundraising, Marketing, Partnerships, etc.	Key Achievements and Goals
Although yoga teachers should be required to have appropriate training, this may not be the case.	Completely informal, but usually one person leads.	None.	Decide on name. Gain access to CJ facility or program. Start yoga classes (pilot or ongoing).
Minimum training standards (e.g., 200-hr YTT), but no specialized training available or required. May have minimal, informal mentoring process.	Clearer organizational structure but often no formal incorporation as 501c3, etc.	Ad hoc, occasional fundraisers. Informal social media presence. No ongoing partnerships. Simple website.	Improve quality and consistency of yoga classes offered. Consider developing population-responsive curriculum.
Yoga teachers required to have specialized training (e.g., 200-hr YTT plus trauma-informed yoga), but organization does not always have dedicated training of its own. Basic mentoring program established.	Formal organization form (501c3, LLC, etc.).	Basic structure for minimal ongoing fundraising in place. Solid social media presence. Exploring partnerships.	Solidify sustainability of organization, start developing in-house teacher training program. Create more-formal evaluation and data-tracking systems, both for programs and operational work such as fundraising.
Teachers required to meet basic requirements and have specialized training developed by and for the organization itself. Ongoing education for teachers and program evaluation.	Formal organization form (501c3, LLC, etc.).	Strong fundraising and marketing operations. Solid partnerships. Database in place for tracking of gifts and relationships.	Sustain operations. Consider expanding via franchising, developing YTT program for the incarcerated, etc.

APPENDIX C: Editor, Contributor, and Reviewer Bios

Bob Altman, RYT-200, serves as treasurer of the Yoga Service Council and was a member of the board of directors from 2013 to 2016. Bob is involved in a number of yoga service–related nonprofits and was cofounder of Centering Youth, an Atlanta-based 501(c)(3) yoga service initiative that brings yoga and mindfulness to young people in the criminal justice system, to those who have been sexually exploited, to the homeless, and to other groups of young people and adults. Bob also has more than 40 years of experience as an attorney, administrator, and judge. He is committed to working with the yoga service community to create sustainable yoga service organizations, as well as to raising awareness of and involvement in yoga service across the nation and beyond.

Susanna Barkataki, MEd, E-YRT, is dedicated to sharing her lineage of yoga, Ayurveda, and mindfulness to bring more harmony, empowerment, and joy into people's lives. She is a writer, speaker, and teacher passionate about self-care, yoga, Ayurveda, social entrepreneurship, and healing justice. She runs a pay-it-forward online meditation program called OM in 2 Bliss and is a cofounder of Be Yoga Pro, a next-level eight-week business training program for yoga teachers. Susanna has served on the board of Yoga Service Council and is a member of the Yoga and Body Image Coalition. She offers bimonthly blogs on yoga, healing, and everyday uplift at www.SusannaBarkataki.com.

Leslie Booker is a Yoga Service Council cofounder and currently serves as an advisor. Passionate about supporting the sustainability of those on the front lines of social change, she co-created the Meditation Working Group of Occupy Wall Street and offers monthly Yoga for ChangeMakers workshops, retreats for refuge and resiliency for activists, and diversity trainings for yoga teachers. Booker gives lectures and workshops on social justice and embodied wisdom to law students, undergraduates, and direct service agencies nationally. She has taught mindfulness and yoga to incarcerated and system-involved youth since 2007. She serves as the director of trainings for Lineage Project and on the faculties of the Prison Mindfulness Institute, Spirit Rock, the Barre Center, and Off the Mat, Into the World.

Bill Brown, PRYT, C-IAYT, RYT-200, is the director of programs for Prison Yoga Project, San Diego. He has brought yoga and mindfulness to San Diego County prisons and jails since 2013 at federal, state, and county facilities. In addition to his service in the criminal justice system, Bill works with a variety of nonprofits to make yoga available to people who might not have access otherwise. Committed to growing the field, Bill particularly enjoys training and mentoring teachers in yoga service and trauma-informed practices. He also maintains a private practice as a Phoenix Rising Yoga Therapy (PRYT) practitioner and group facilitator, specializing in working with survivors of trauma.

Denise Davidson has served as the warden of a women's prison since 2013. Her career in corrections started in 1987 as a correctional officer. She has worked in four different men's facilities at all custody levels for 26 years. She was promoted through the ranks with her first appointment to warden in 2012 at a Community Corrections facility. Denise is a longtime member of the American Correctional Association and a recent graduate of the Warden Exchange Program with Prison Fellowship Ministries, which focuses on transformational leadership and transforming prisons.

Toni DeMarco, MS, MFT, is a clinical services manager for Behavioral Health and Recovery Services (BHRS) Youth Division, San Mateo County Health System. She manages three large teams in the youth division: the Juvenile Probation BHRS team, the Child Welfare BHRS team, and the Prenatal to Three BHRS team. She is also the site coordinator for San Mateo County's Neurosequential Model of Therapeutics (NMT) Implementation and Training program. A licensed therapist for more than 25 years, Toni has worked in both the public and nonprofit sectors as a clinician, supervisor, manager, and educator, focusing on trauma and its generational impact on families and children. A certified Phase II NMT Trainer and a certified Master Trainer in the LivingWorks ASIST (applied suicide intervention skills training) model, Toni has spent her career working with issues of youth suicide, self-harm, trauma, and recovery.

Marshawn Devon Feltus, a Chicago west-side native, was sentenced to 38 years in the Illinois Department of Corrections just shy of his 18th birthday. While incarcerated, he was introduced to his first yoga class. Later, he became a co-instructor and helped train more than 800 men in yoga. In 2013, Marshawn opened the first yoga studio in Chicago's Austin community: ACT Yoga, which stands for awareness, change, and triumph. His mission is to fulfill his life's assignment to teach, touch, and transmit awareness, change, and triumph, particularly but not exclusively among urban teens and incarcerated youth and adults. Marshawn has served on the board of Westside Health Authority, is president of the We Are Light organization, and is an advisor to the Yoga Service Council. Marshawn's many accomplishments include: certification in crisis-prevention intervention and conflict resolution, Red Cross CPR certification, training as a youth mentor, yoga instructor certification, training in mindfulness meditation, and certification as a public health peer educator.

Mary Lynn Fitton, RN, MS, FNP, in 2005, founded The Art of Yoga Project, a nonprofit offering trauma-informed, gender-responsive yoga and creative arts curricula to justice-involved girls as an integral part of their healing and rehabilitation. Mary Lynn received her master's in science and her family nurse practitioner degree at the University of California–San Francisco, with specialties in neuroscience and women's and adolescent health care. She is an international speaker and a train-the-trainer for the Child Trauma Academy's Neurosequential Model of Therapeutics. A certified yoga teacher since 1998 and founding member of the Yoga Service Council, her work has been featured in *The Washington Post, Yoga Journal, The San Francisco Examiner, The Mercury News,* and *The International Journal of Yoga Therapy,* as well as on NPR and *The Huffington Post.*

James Fox, MA, is the founder/director of Prison Yoga Project with 15 years of experience providing trauma-informed, mindfulness-based yoga practices to adult prisoners and at-risk youth. He is the author of *Yoga: A Path for Healing and Recovery*, a book that has been distributed free of charge to 18,000 prisoners who have requested it. His prison yoga program, originally established at San Quentin in 2002, has been replicated in more than 200 jails and prisons throughout the United States, as well as in Mexico, Canada, and Europe. James has teaching experience in restorative justice practices, including violence prevention and offender accountability classes for prisoners. He has been a recipient of U.S. State Department grants to train people involved in prisoner rehabilitation in Central America.

Jennifer Cohen Harper MA, E-RYT, RCYT, is the board president of the Yoga Service Council, as well as one of its founding members. Jenn originated the Yoga Service Conference and was the coeditor of *Best Practices for Yoga in Schools*, the first of the YSC Best Practices guides. As the founder and director of Little Flower Yoga, serving more than 10,000 students a year, Jenn is a leading voice in the children's yoga and mindfulness community. She is also the author of *Little Flower Yoga for Kids: A Yoga and Mindfulness Program to Help Your Child Improve Attention and Emotional Balance.* Jenn provides therapeutic classes to children and families, as well as continuing education to mental health and education professionals. Her work has been featured in *The New York Times, International Journal of Yoga Therapy, Publishers Weekly,* and *Yoga Journal,* and endorsed by thought leaders including Daniel Siegel, Sharon Salzberg, and Congressman Tim Ryan.

Gabrielle Prisco, MA, Esq., is the executive director of Lineage Project, which brings mindfulness programs to incarcerated and vulnerable youth to help them manage stress, build inner strength, and cultivate compassion. Lineage also trains youth-serving organizations to develop trauma-informed, mindful cultures. Gabrielle previously served as director of the Juvenile Justice Project at the Correctional Association of New York; a Legal Aid Society attorney for children; a Brennan Fellow at the ACLU; and the Derrick Bell Fellow at NYU Law. She holds a JD cum laude from NYU Law, an MA from the University of

Alabama, and a BS magna cum laude from Vanderbilt University. She authored *When the Cure Makes You Ill: Seven Core Principles to Change the Course of Youth Justice* and gave the TEDx talk "On Canaries, Love and Justice."

Carol Horton, PhD, is the author or editor of five books: *Yoga PhD, 21st Century Yoga, Best Practices for Yoga with Veterans, Best Practices for Yoga in the Criminal Justice System,* and *Race and the Making of American Liberalism.* She serves as vice president of the Yoga Service Council and is a cofounder of Chicago's Socially Engaged Yoga Network. Carol completed her foundational yoga teacher training with Ana Forrest and studied trauma-informed yoga with James Fox (Prison Yoga Project) and Mark Lilly (Street Yoga). She has taught yoga in Cook County Jail, a drop-in center for homeless women, a residential foster care facility, a community health center, and several independent studios. An ex–political science professor, she holds a doctorate from the University of Chicago.

Michael Huggins, MBA, E-RYT-200, is the founder of the Transformation Yoga Project and author of *Going Om: A CEO's Journey from a Prison Facility to Spiritual Tranquility.* Transformation Yoga Project serves people impacted by trauma, addiction, and incarceration through trauma-sensitive, mindfulness-based yoga. Mike has been practicing yoga since 2003. He left the corporate world to focus on applying yoga practices for addiction recovery and trauma-related issues. Mike is in on the board of several nonprofits. He has a bachelor of science degree from Villanova University and a master of business administration from the Wharton School at the University of Pennsylvania.

Jill Weiss Ippolito, RYT, became a yoga teacher to share the healing that saved her life. Formerly a system-involved youth, as an incarcerated adult she turned her life around with yoga and went on to complete over 900 hours of yoga teacher training. In 2011, Jill founded the non-profit UpRising Yoga (URY) and began teaching yoga life skill classes in youth detention facilities, group homes, hospitals, schools, camps, homeless shelters, and underserved communities. Jill educates hundreds of yoga instructors, childcare providers, mental health professionals, and educators through her domestic and international Yoga For Healing Trauma (YFHT) trainings, which have been incorporated into the mandatory curriculum for Los Angeles probation officers. Jill serves as a leader and advocate dedicated to reforming prison and probation culture and changing lives for the better through yoga.

De Jur Jones, C-IAYT, RYT-200, is a Los Angeles–based, Loyola Marymount University–certified Yoga Therapist under the guidance of Dr. Larry Payne. Her interest to teach yoga off of the mainstream path was sparked by an article on Prison Yoga Project's James Fox, with whom she's trained and mentored by. She has been certified by Rev. Jivana Heyman as an Accessible Yoga Teacher and Ambassador, and is a graduate of Julian Walker and Hala Khouri's trauma-informed 200-hour yoga teacher training program. De Jur teaches trauma-informed, accessible yoga therapy to special-needs populations, maximum-security males, and women in California jails and prisons. She also holds classes with youth in the juvenile justice system, juvenile halls, probation camps, and justice staff around Los Angeles County.

Sue Jones created yogaHOPE to facilitate access to yoga and mindfulness education for women experiencing debilitating life transitions such as establishing independence from domestic violence, finding self-sufficiency from homelessness, and recovering from drug addiction or sexual assault. yogaHOPE's powerfully effective TIMBo (trauma-informed mind-body) program incorporates a research-based curriculum focused on how mind-body practices support long-term traumatic stress recovery. Through yogaHOPE's peer-to-peer and train-the-trainer model, women across the globe have been empowered to bring TIMBo to their own communities, creating an exponential culture of healing and empowerment. yogaHOPE has trained TIMBo leaders in correctional facilities, homeless shelters, substance abuse treatment centers, and high schools throughout the United States. Global TIMBo communities include Haiti, Kenya, and Iran. TIMBo for organizational well-being is in the early stages of partnership and development.

Hala Khouri, MA, SEP, E-RYT, is one of the founders of Off the Mat, Into the World, a nonprofit that offers educational and leadership training for yoga practitioners who want to bridge yoga, social justice, and community engagement.

She is a somatic experiencing practitioner specializing in working with trauma in her private practice, as well as a yoga teacher and yoga teacher trainer Hala also works with direct service providers, training them to be trauma informed. She has a master's in counseling psychology from Pacifica Graduate Institute and is currently working on a PhD in community psychology, liberation studies, and eco-psychology.

Anneke Lucas, EW-RYT-500, founded Liberation Prison Yoga (LPY) in 2014 and serves as its executive director. LPY works with an average of 35 trained volunteer teachers to offer more than 20 weekly trauma-informed yoga programs at Rikers Island, the Manhattan Detention Complex, Bedford Hills Maximum-Security Prison, Taconic State Medium-Security Prison, and Wallkill Medium-Security Prison, in New York State. LPY additionally runs jail-based programs for transgender women, those in drug rehab, and severely mentally ill women; studio-based weekly community classes for formerly incarcerated students; and programs at reentry facilities. A survivor of child sex trafficking and extreme violence, Anneke has used elements of her own 30-year healing journey to develop programs based on how she would have wished to be treated in her young adult life. Currently, she is designing a 200-hour Yoga Alliance–registered teacher training for Liberation Prison Yoga, focusing on bringing yoga to traumatized populations. She's writing a book about her healing journey, *Seeds Beneath the Snow: Post-Traumatic Growth and Purpose in Dark Times.*

Sarahjoy Marsh MA, E-RYT-500, yoga teacher and author, is a vibrant, compassionate catalyst for transformation. Her teachings are informed by her extensive Eastern and Western studies, including transpersonal counseling, art therapy, interpersonal neurobiology, the psychology of yoga, Ayurveda, and rehabilitative yoga. Her book *Hunger, Hope, and Healing: A Yoga Approach to Reclaiming Your Relationship with Your Body and Food* outlines her unique approach: integrating powerful yoga and mindfulness tools with modern-day psychological modalities for an effective and comprehensive approach to healing. Committed to supporting marginalized populations and using yoga for social justice, Sarahjoy founded Living Yoga and the DAYA Foundation. You can find her at www.sarahjoyyoga.com.

Mary Ellen Mastrorilli, PhD, is an associate professor of the practice and associate chair of the applied social sciences department at Boston University's Metropolitan College. Prior to joining the faculty, she spent 24 years working in the correctional system in Massachusetts and Rhode Island, holding a variety of positions such as captain, director of training, and prison superintendent. She is the recipient of the Professional Excellence Award from the Correctional Association of Massachusetts and the Breaking the Glass Ceiling Award from the National Center for Women and Policing. Mary Ellen earned her bachelor's degree from the University of Massachusetts in Boston, master's degree in public administration from Suffolk University, and PhD at Northeastern University. Her areas of research interest are prison programming, community corrections, and female offenders. Mary Ellen is manager of Safe Prisons, where she does consulting on the prevention, detection, and elimination of prison rape.

Kath Meadows, MA, E-RYT-500, is director of Women Prisoner Initiatives for Prison Yoga Project. Kath's principal interest is in bringing gender-sensitive, trauma-informed yoga practices to the incarcerated population. She has been teaching yoga and mindfulness in prisons since 2010. Starting from one weekly class, she has expanded prison yoga programs in Maryland to multiple weekly classes for men and women at state and federal facilities, and she has grown a community of prison yoga teachers to whom she provides ongoing support and training. Recognizing the demand for materials that acknowledge the specific needs of the female prisoner, Kath wrote *A Woman's Practice: Healing from the Heart*, an accessible guide to the healing benefits of yoga for women in all bodies. More than 2,000 copies have been sent free of charge to prisoners in the United States and overseas. Continually looking for ways to expand access to yoga in prisons, Kath has developed and implemented a pioneering Yoga Alliance–registered 200-hour YTT for women prisoners, in collaboration with The Yoga Center of Columbia, Maryland.

Brianne Murphy Cerdán, BA, E-RYT-200, graduated from Temple University with dual undergraduate degrees in religion and visual anthropology. Since completing her 200-hour certification in 2013, she has focused primarily on continuing education in trauma sensitivity for youth and adults, yoga service, and the intersectionality of social justice, with more than 400 hours of continuing education. She is a trained facilitator in the Inside Out: Prison Exchange Program Methodology and in Transformative Social Theory's Intergroup Dialogue techniques. She has presented the benefits of trauma-sensitive yoga at several local justice-oriented events, including a TEDx organized by the Pennsylvania Department of Corrections in 2016. Brianne leads Transformation Yoga Project's Criminal Justice Training, co-facilitates yoga teacher training and continuing education in prisons and justice-oriented institutions, and directs and manages programs for system-involved youths and adults.

Danielle Rousseau, PhD, LMHC, is an assistant professor at Boston University. She is a licensed therapist and certified yoga teacher. Danielle's professional focus has been in trauma services and gender advocacy. She is a social justice researcher and practitioner. For more than a decade, Dr. Rousseau has worked in the field of forensic mental health as a therapist in correctional facilities as well as in the community doing crisis response and victim advocacy. Her research, teaching, and practice focus on the areas of justice, trauma, gender, mental health, and mindfulness. She is an advocate of integrative, holistic approaches that support embodied self-care.

Charlene A. Sams, E-RYT, CRYT, affectionately known by her spiritual name, Amina Naru, is a member of the Yoga Service Council board of directors, where she serves as secretary. She works as a yoga instructor, workshop facilitator, owner of Wilmington's Posh Yoga studio, and YSC Best Practices project manager. Charlene is the first black woman to implement curriculum-based yoga and mindfulness programs for all of the youth detention centers in the state of Delaware, with the assistance of Chief Judge of Family Court, the Honorable Chandlee Khun. She has trained with master teachers including Johnny Gillespie (Empowered Yoga), James Fox (Prison Yoga Project), B. K. Bose (Niroga Institute), and Jennifer Cohen Harper (Little Flower Yoga). Charlene's mission is to open a residential yoga and mindfulness school for youth in Delaware and expand that model to other states, while supporting the development of yoga programs in every prison facility in the United States.

Jessica Stolley, MS, LMHP, LDAC, is a dually credentialed clinician. Her clinical focus includes mindfulness, social skills, stress reduction, peer support, victim impact, restorative justice, and reintegration/transitional programming for populations on parole or within 0 to 3 years of sentence completion. She also works with issues of adolescent behavior (cutting, anxiety, depression, and academic performance), couples therapy, severe mental illness, antisocial and borderline personality disorders, and parent-child relationships. Her approach is trauma-informed and gender-sensitive, and draws from modalities including cognitive behavioral therapy, dialectical behavior therapy, and solutions focused therapy. Jessica partners with university-based research programs to support the growth and development of future community transition programs. She prides herself on the art of building good relationships and doing the right thing.

Laura Sygrove, RYT-500, MSW (in progress), is the cofounder and executive director of New Leaf Foundation (www.newleafyoga.org), a Toronto, Canada-based organization that has been serving youth in marginalized communities since 2007. She is a certified yoga and mindfulness-yoga teacher with a focus on trauma-informed practice and youth engagement. Laura has studied with David Emerson, Lineage Project, Street Yoga, MBA Project, Off the Mat Into the World, Hart Lazer, Bessel van der Kolk, John Briere, and Jane Clapp. Laura has trained more than 200 yoga teachers in trauma-informed best practices, and she is a faculty member of the innovative Yoga Detour teacher training. In addition to overseeing New Leaf Foundation's 30 long-term yoga service programs, she has facilitated yoga and mindfulness-based programs with young men in custody settings for a decade. Laura is currently pursuing her master's degree in social work with a specialization in indigenous trauma and resilience, at the University of Toronto.

Kathryn Monti Thomas, E-RYT, RCYT, is the executive director of Yoga 4 Change. After being medically separated from the United States Navy in which she served as a Naval Aviator, she began studying to become a yoga teacher through the Yoga School of Kailua. Upon moving to Jacksonville, Florida, she witnessed the need for mental, emotional, and physical healing in her new community and started Yoga 4 Change to fill this void. Kathryn has training in multiple disciplines including power yoga, chair yoga, *hatha* yoga, and *yoga nidra*. She is an E-RYT-500 and Certified Baptiste Teacher. Kathryn formerly sat on the Board of the Yoga Service Council, where she served as project manager and contributor both to this work and its predecessor, *Best Practices for Yoga with Veterans*. She resides in Florida with her husband, daughter, and two Labrador Retrievers.

Rosa Vissers, MFA, E-YT-500, sees movement as a powerful pathway to reclaim our beauty, resilience, and connection—to ourselves and each other. She is the executive director of Yoga Behind Bars (YBB, www.yogabehindbars.org), a Seattle-based nonprofit offering trauma-informed yoga to incarcerated youth and adults. Rosa has shared the practice of yoga with incarcerated people for many years and trained hundreds of others to do the same. Under her leadership, YBB has more than doubled its programs to include 17 prisons and jails in Washington state. In 2015, Rosa spearheaded YBB's launch of its yoga teacher trainings behind bars and presented a TEDx talk on yoga in prisons. Rosa has an extensive background as an international dance artist and holds a BFA and an MFA in modern dance.

Kimberleigh Weiss-Lewit, MA, RYT 500, CD/CDT, is Liberation Prison Yoga's director of Women's Services. She also serves as an LPY board member and co-leads its trauma-informed teacher training. Kim provides support for prenatal and postpartum yoga programs, as well as breastfeeding and new parent support, at Rikers Island in New York City. She is a registered yoga teacher, certified prenatal yoga teacher, La Leche League leader, birth doula, birth doula trainer, and part of the teaching staff and teacher training team at the Hudson Yoga Project in Hoboken, New Jersey. After obtaining an MA in drama therapy from New York University, she began prison-based work more than a decade ago with the nonprofit Rehabilitation Through the Arts, serving people in both men's and women's prisons in New York State.

REFERENCES

Alexander, M. (2012). *The new jim crow: Mass incarceration in the age of colorblindness*. New York: The New Press

Bureau of Justice Statistics (BJS). (n.d.). FAQ detail: What is the difference between probation and parole? Retrieved from https://www.bjs.gov/index.cfm?ty=qa&iid=324

Bullock, B. G. (n.d.). The many health benefits of yoga: What does the research say? Part II. *Yoga U Online*. Retrieved from https://www.yogauonline.com/yogau-wellness-blog/many-health-benefits-yoga-what-does-research-say-part-ii

Cartmell, P. (n.d.). State prison system vs. federal prison system. Retrieved June 19, 2017, from http://peopleof.oureverydaylife.com/state-vs-federal-prison-system-11806.html

Centers for Disease Control and Prevention (CDC). (2016, April 5). Child abuse and neglect: Consequences. Retrieved from https://www.cdc.gov/violenceprevention/childmaltreatment/consequences.html

Center for Effective Public Policy (CEPP). (2015). Who collaborates in criminal justice? Retrieved June 26, 2017, from http://www.collaborativejustice.org/who.htm

Childress, T. & Cohen Harper, J. (2016, February). What is yoga service? A working definition. Retrieved from https://yogaservicecouncil.org/community-resource-papers

Child Welfare Information Gateway (CWIF). (2015). Mandatory reporters of child abuse and neglect. Children's Bureau/ACYF/ACF/HHS. Retrieved from https://www.childwelfare.gov/pubPDFs/manda.pdf

Common Sense for Drug Policy (CSDP). (n.d.). Drug courts. In D. A. McVay (ed.) DrugWarFacts.org. Retrieved June 19, 2017, from http://www.drugwarfacts.org/cms/Drug_Courts#sthash.lk7xPDKz.dpuf

Cook County Department of Corrections (CCDC). (n.d.). Retrieved June 19, 2017, from http://www.cookcountysheriff.com/doc/doc_main.html

Development Services Group. (2014). Commercial sexual exploitation of children/sex trafficking. (Literature review.) Washington, D.C.: Office of Juvenile Justice and Delinquency Prevention. Retrieved from https://www.ojjdp.gov/mpg/litreviews/CSECSexTrafficking.pdf

DrugRehab.com. (n.d.). Court-ordered treatment. Retrieved June 19, 2017, from https://www.drugrehab.com/treatment/court-ordered/

Epstein, R., & González, T. (2017). Gender and trauma: Somatic interventions for girls in juvenile justice: Implications for policy and practice. Washington, D.C.: Center on Poverty and Inequality, Georgetown Law. Retrieved from http://www.law.georgetown.edu/academics/centers-institutes/poverty-inequality/upload/gender-and-trauma.pdf

Emerson, D., & Hopper, E. (2011). *Overcoming trauma through yoga: Reclaiming your body*. Berkeley, CA: North Atlantic Books

Gates, A., Artiga, S., & Rudowitz, R. (2014, September 5). Health coverage and care for the adult criminal justice–involved population. The Henry J. Kaiser Family Foundation. Retrieved from http://kff.org/uninsured/issue-brief/health-coverage-and-care-for-the-adult-criminal-justice-involved-population/

Global Detention Project. (2016, May). United States immigration detention profile. Retrieved June 19, 2017, from https://www.globaldetentionproject.org/countries/americas/united-states

Haney, C. (2001, December 1). The psychological impact of incarceration: Implications for post-prison adjustment. U.S. Department of Health & Human Services, Office of the Assistant Secretary for Planning and Evaluation. Retrieved from https://aspe.hhs.gov/basic-report/psychological-impact-incarceration-implications-post-prison-adjustment#II

Hickman, B. (2015, April 3). Inmate. Prisoner. Other. Discussed. What to call incarcerated people: Your feedback. Retrieved from https://www.themarshallproject.org/2015/04/03/inmate-prisoner-other-discussed#.CBEtABoGo

Horton, C., Banitt, S. P., Bechtel, L., Danylchuk, L., Huggins, M., & Eggleston, P. S. (2016). *Best practices for yoga with veterans*. New York: YSC/Omega Books.

Institute of Medicine and National Research Council (IM/NRC). (2001). The juvenile justice system. In J. McCord, C. Spatz Widom, & N. A. Crowell (Eds.) *Juvenile crime, juvenile justice*. Washington, D.C.: The National Academies Press. https://doi.org/10.17226/9747. Retrieved from https://www.nap.edu/read/9747/chapter/7

Jackman, T. (2016, May 18). Mass reduction of California prison population didn't cause rise in crime, two studies find. *The Washington Post*. Retrieved from https://www.washingtonpost.com/news/true-crime/wp/2016/05/18/mass-release-of-california-prisoners-didnt-cause-rise-in-crime-two-studies-find/?utm_term=.f64b29541c8d

Jackson, A. (2009, December). *Principles for safe, positive physical contact*. Unpublished manuscript. Berry Street Childhood Institute: Richmond, Victoria, Australia

Jull, S. (n.d.). What are the different types of correctional institutions? Retrieved from http://peopleof.oureverydaylife.com/different-types-correctional-institutions-11845.html

van Dernoot Lipsky, L., & Burk, C. (2009). *Trauma stewardship: An everyday guide to caring for self while caring for others*. San Francisco: Berrett-Koehler

Lopez, O. (2014, May 27). Prison officers need help, but they won't ask for it. *Newsweek*. Retrieved from http://www.newsweek.com/2014/06/06/prison-officers-need-help-they-wont-ask-it-252439.html

McLaughlin, M., Pettus-Davis, C., Brown, D., Veeh, C., & Renn, T. (2016, October). *The Economic Burden of Incarceration in the U.S.*, Working paper no. AJI072016. Institute for Advancing Justice Research and Innovation, George Warren Brown School of Social Work.). St. Louis, MO: Washington University. Retrieved from https://advancingjustice.wustl.edu/ SiteCollectionDocuments/The%20Economic%20Burden%20of%20Incarceration%20in%20 the%20US.pdf

Meyer, I. H., Flores, A. R., Stemple, L., Romero, A. P., Wilson, B. D. M., & Herman, J. L. (2017, February). Incarceration rates and traits of sexual minorities in the United States: National inmate survey, 2011–2012. *American Journal of Public Health, 107*(2): 234–240. Retrieved from http://williamsinstitute.law.ucla.edu/wp-content/uploads/Meyer_Final_Proofs.LGB_.In_.pdf

Michon, J. K. (n.d.). Juvenile court: An overview. Retrieved from http://www.nolo.com/legal-encyclopedia/juvenile-court-overview-32222.html

Minton, T., & Zeng, Z. (2016, December). Jail inmates in 2015. Bureau of Justice Statistics Bulletin. Retrieved from https://www.bjs.gov/content/pub/pdf/ji15.pdf

Muirhead, J., & Fortune, C. (2016, May–June). Yoga in prisons: A review of the literature. *Aggression and Violent Behavior* 28: 57–63. Retrieved from http://www.sciencedirect.com/ science/article/pii/S1359178916300246

National Child Traumatic Stress Network (NCTSN). (2017). Complex trauma. Retrieved from http://nctsn.org/trauma-types/complex-trauma

Perry, B. D. (2006). The neurosequential model of therapeutics: Applying principles of neuroscience to clinical work with traumatized and maltreated children. In N. B. Webb (Ed.) *Working with Traumatized Youth in Child Welfare*. New York: Guilford.

Remen, R. N. (n.d.). In the service of life. Retrieved from http://learningcommunity.us/ documents/IntheServiceofLife.pdf

Rogers, C. R. (1986). Client-centered approach to therapy. In I. L. Kutash & A. Wolf (Eds.) *Psychotherapist's casebook: Theory and technique in practice*. San Francisco: Jossey-Bass

Sentencing Project. (n.d.). Criminal justice facts: State-by-state data. Retrieved February 2, 2016, from http://www.sentencingproject.org/the-facts/#rankings?dataset-option=SIR

Sentencing Project. (2017, June). Fact sheet: Trends in U.S. corrections. Retrieved February 2, 2016, from http://sentencingproject.org/wp-content/uploads/2016/01/Trends-in-US-Corrections.pdf

Sentencing Project. (2015, November 30). Incarcerated women and girls. Retrieved June 23, 2017, from http://www.sentencingproject.org/publications/incarcerated-women-and-girls/

Shapiro, D. (2011, November 2). Banking on bondage: Private prisons and mass incarceration. American Civil Liberties Union. Retrieved from https://www.aclu.org/ banking-bondage-private-prisons-and-mass-incarceration

Sherts, M. (2009). *Conscious communication: How to establish healthy relationships and resolve conflict peacefully while maintaining independence: A language of connection.* Minneapolis, MN: Langdon Street Press.

Swavola, E., Riley, K., & Subramanian, R. (2016, August). Overlooked: Women and jails in an era of reform. Retrieved from https://www.vera.org/publications/overlooked-women-and-jails-report

van der Kolk, B. (2014). *The body keeps the score: Brain, mind, and body in the healing of trauma.* New York, NY: Viking

Viorst, M. (2017). Former inmates perceptions of the prison yoga project. Undergraduate Honors Thesis, Department of Sociology, University of Colorado, Boulder. Retrieved from http://scholar.colorado.edu/honr_theses/1494

Wagner, P. (2015, August 14). Jails matter. But who is listening? Prison Policy Initiative. Retrieved from https://www.prisonpolicy.org/blog/2015/08/14/jailsmatter/

Wagner, P., & Rabuy, B. (2017, March 14). Mass Incarceration: The Whole Pie 2017. Prison Policy Initiative. Retrieved from https://www.prisonpolicy.org/reports/pie2017.html?utm_source=nl-atlantic-daily-082817&%3Bsilverid=MzU4NzU0NTQ1OTU5S0

Walmsley, R. (2015). World population prison list (11th ed.). World prison brief. Institute for Criminal Policy Research. Retrieved from http://www.prisonstudies.org/sites/default/files/resources/downloads/world_prison_population_list_11th_edition_0.pdf

Whitten, L. (2012, October 5). Addressing trauma among incarcerated people. National Institute of Corrections. Retrieved from http://community.nicic.gov/blogs/mentalhealth/archive/2012/10/05/addressing-trauma-among-incarcerated-people.aspx

Yalom, I. D. (1985). *The theory and practice of group psychotherapy.* New York: Basic Books

Made in the USA
Columbia, SC
12 December 2017